The Filmic Moment

Ralph J. Amelio

Pflaum Publishing, Dayton, Ohio

I would like to thank the following people for their help and cooperation in this project: Charles Benton, Doug Lemza, and Gale Livengood, all of Films Incorporated; Phyllis Davis and John Mostacci of Willowbrook High School; Stuart M. Kaminsky and Paddy Whannel of Northwestern University; and Dorothy.

© 1975 by Ralph J. Amelio

Library of Congress Catalog Card Number 75–2653
ISBN 0-8278-0268-4
Book Design by Joe Loverti

To Ralph and Viktusia

Contents

Chapter One

Purpose of the Book

The purpose of this book is threefold:
- To provide information explaining and supporting another tool for the study of film—film extracts;
- To document work on a cooperative film project involving a major film distributor (Films Incorporated, of Skokie, Illinois), three teachers (Paddy Whannel and Stuart Kaminsky, from Northwestern University, Evanston, Illinois; and myself, from Willowbrook High School, Villa Park, Illinois), and a book publisher (Pflaum Publishing, of Dayton, Ohio);
- To encourage both a dialogue among film teachers to promote experimentation with film extract material and a willingness among other film distributors to provide additional film extracts. (In regard to this last purpose, I have included in Chapter Four suggestions based both on the extracts that now exist as well as on those which, if they existed, could be used to advantage in film study courses.)

Background of the Project

Charles Benton, of Films Incorporated, asked Paddy Whannel (formerly of the British Film Institute and now at Northwestern University as chairman of the Film Division), Stuart M. Kaminsky (assistant professor of film at Northwestern), and me (as a representative of high school film course teaching) to work on a project in extracting film. The three teachers' duties were to view as many of the feature films as Films Incorporated had available, to select extracts from them, and to provide supporting rationales. Since Films Incorporated has a fine collection of American films, we decided to choose the extracted films from six of the major genres (types)[1] of American film: the Western, comedy, science fiction, horror, musical, and gangster films. Not all the films in the Films Incorporated collection were available for extracting because some of the major companies were unable to grant permission to cut a film for various reasons: either the company did not have complete rights; the film was too contemporary; or the film or parts of it were being shown on television.

Once the genres were agreed on, the teachers began viewing and reviewing the films. Within six months we viewed more than 200 feature films. In many cases the feature, as well as the extract from it, was analyzed three or four times; at least half of the films and their extracts were used in high school and college classes at Willowbrook and Northwestern. (National testing of the total package of extracts has been proposed through the cooperation of Films Incorporated and the National Association of Media Educators.) As each genre was selected, the teachers proposed at least four films that they believed were most representative (of those available for extracting) of each genre. After the films were viewed by each teacher separately, we compared our reactions, discussed scenes and sequences from each film, and agreed upon at least one possible extract from each film.

We eventually whittled the number of extracts down to what Films Incorporated had suggested as an initial program—two films per genre, plus one or two backup extracts in case permission for certain films could not be given. In some cases, prior to and during the selection process, we tried tentative extracts in our own classes. Had there been more time for the project, we would have preferred to experiment with all the extracts and to document the lessons. We await this type of activity from teachers in the field as soon as the films become available for distribution. Despite the diverse training and background of each of the teachers, however, we were able to agree upon the selections with little or no difficulty and a great amount of intellectual interchange.

When the excerpts had been marked for extracting by the three teachers, Films Incorporated's production crew then cut a print of each film and added its logo, titling, and credits. We pro-

[1] See Chapter Four, pages 28 and following, for a detailed definition of genre.

vided a brief rationale for each selection, and Films Incorporated developed its own advertising and sales package.

From the very beginning of this project, Jack Heher of Pflaum, publisher of two previous film books by me, was advised of and interested in the use of film extracts as a teaching aid. Professor Stuart Kaminsky had nearly completed his scholarly manuscript on American film genres; as a result, Mr. Heher also became interested in his book. Paddy Whannel, co-author of the influential *The Popular Arts*, had considerable experience in selecting and using film extracts in England for the British Film Institute. I was teaching a course using different approaches to film study, including the genre approach. Thus, Films Incorporated became the catalyst for arranging a meeting among the various participants: the distributor, his staff, the three teachers, and the publisher.

As of now, the result of the project is the existence of 12 extracts, representing six film genres, and accompanied by study guides developed by Films Incorporated's staff as well as cassette tapes of Professor Kaminsky's lectures on them, in addition to two books—this one and *American Film Genres* by Stuart M. Kaminsky. If this project is successful in its educational and commerical aspects, Films Incorporated is willing to continue to develop other film extracts.

Chapter Two

Rationale for Film Study

In thousands of high schools and colleges across the United States, film programs and courses are mushrooming; some of them include instruction in filmmaking, but most involve the understanding and development of a critical awareness of an exciting popular art form. Film, as one of the new humanities, is now accepted into many innovative curricula—and rightly so, for various reasons.

● First, though film does not yet possess the historical and traditional weight of music, literature, or the plastic arts, it is now regarded as a major art form because it can not only synthesize these older art forms into a vibrant experience but also create its own aesthetics for a contemporary society. William Arrowsmith, in his article "Film as Educator," has said:

> "What the novel was to the nineteenth century, the film might be to the twentieth: the genre, the only genre wholly congenial to the majority of a culture." [1]

In film's brief 70-year history, it already has paralleled the work of such great nineteenth-century novelists as Twain, Hawthorne, Dickens, Hugo, Dostoevski, Turgenev, and Tolstoy. It has created its own geniuses for a wider audience: Ingmar Bergman, Federico Fellini, François Truffaut, Satyajit Ray, Jean Renoir, Akira Kuro-

---

[1] William Arrowsmith, "Film as Educator," *Journal of Aesthetic Education*, Vol. 3, No. 3 (July, 1969), p. 78.

sawa, Sergei Eisenstein, Orson Welles, Howard Hawks, John Ford, Buster Keaton, Charlie Chaplin, and many more. Why should schools not reap the advantages of the situation which film critic Stanley Kauffmann describes: "Film is the art for which there is the greatest spontaneous appetite in America at present"?

Just as we readily accept and teach the literary versions of classical themes indigenous to America by such brilliant writers as Twain, Fitzgerald, Hemingway, and Mailer, so also might we consider the filmic treatment—classical, popular, and mythic—of American themes by such directors as John Ford, Henry King, Roger Corman, and Howard Hawks. No longer can film be dismissed as "mere" entertainment only. All countries subject film—directly or indirectly—to censorship control, a measure of the importance it is credited with as a message bearer. The fact that millions of people have viewed film, and continue to do so in the theater, on television, and now in the schools, indicates that film as one of the popular arts deserves serious attention—at least as a mirror of the social and cultural attitudes of a people, and even possibly as a catalyst for social action and influence on behavior and public opinion. Siegfried Kracauer, author of *From Caligari to Hitler: A Psychological History of the German Film,* said: "Films help mass attitudes on condition that these attitudes have already begun to change." The study of film is not an attempt to supplant other curricula, especially reading; instead, the stress should be on integrating the study of film and other mass media into the curriculum as a logical requirement for a generation nurtured (if not massaged and manipulated) by the media.

● A second reason for including film study in the curriculum centers on the fact that since young people in their teens and twenties comprise the vast majority of the film audience, educators are beginning to realize the appeal and relevance that film has generated. How many students voluntarily attend a ballet, concert, art show, opera, or dramatic play? Compare the answer to that question with the numbers who regularly view films. Sixty-five percent of today's film audience is 24 years old or younger. For every book the average college student reads, he views 20 films. While it is unfortunate that the older humanities are not being supported by today's youth, the glaring fact remains: students *are* viewing films, both good and bad ones—and for many, the film represents their only substantial experience not only with an art form, but all too often with information itself. The schools possess a marvelous opportunity to apply the poet Horace's advice of "dulce et utile" (delight and usefulness) to film study for students. Most students enjoy film; motivating them to understand and appreciate film on other levels—cognitive, affective, critical, and aesthetic—can be effectively achieved. Just as other cultural experiences are brought to the schools in the areas of music, art, ballet, and drama for the students to broaden their artistic experiences, so also can film be shown in the school.

● Third: today, especially with the proliferation of media which can manipulate their audiences in social, political, economic, artistic, and personal areas, the schools must provide their students with an opportunity to "become"—to realize who they are as individuals—and to understand and criticize both the messages and the media. The fact that television is practically a surrogate parent and electronic pacifier for millions of pre-school children should be an initial indicator that students should have some formal training in visual rhetoric. While it may be comforting to parents that such fine shows as *Sesame Street, Zoom,* and *Misterogers* are viewed by over nine million of the twelve million children under five in the United States, many other parents retain as their resident baby sitter programs sated with mayhem and violence. These children are being nurtured in an environment which their parents have neither created nor controlled.

The output of feature films comprises more than 75 percent of the total television time in all countries and has considerable ideological impact on the television audience as well. The fact that viewing television and film is essentially a one-way activity, with all the work being passively absorbed by the receiver, should alert teachers and parents to the need not only to view and review these experiences carefully but also to discuss these experiences. How many parents fulfill this duty? Obviously, the necessity falls to the schools—already overcrowded, underbudgeted, understaffed with qualified media teachers, and structurally not designed for comprehensive mass media programs (poor acoustics, ineffective blackout curtains, no projection booths). Nevertheless, improvements in each of these negative aspects are being effected as the schools recognize their obligation to help students attain a thorough understanding and critical discrimination of the medium so closely allied to their culture. Such training is a necessity for a student's personal development, awareness, and appreciation of his environment, of others, and of himself.

Film Study Materials

Compared to the recent past, growing quantities of both print and non-print materials are now available for teaching about the film. These materials include the ever-increasing scholarly articles, study guide sheets, periodicals, film catalogs, books, and a wide variety of films: short films, documentaries, animation. Of special significance, however, is the feature film—the form most widely recognized and seen by the young audience, and the form in which the major artists of the cinema have worked and developed their ideas and styles (although several short films by feature-directors are also worth serious attention: Roman Polanski's *Two Men and a Wardrobe*, François Truffaut's *Les Mistons*, John Huston's *Battle, of San Pietro*, George Lucas' *THX 1138*, Noel Black's *Skater-Dater*, and Martin Scorsese's *The Big Shave).* Any course which aims to connect with the students' normal experience and to introduce them to the diverse achievements of cinema at its best must include—if not stress—the serious viewing and discussing of feature films. Because of limited budgets, rising rental costs of films, and problems with school time schedules, however, a teacher will always be restricted as to the number and variety of feature films he can use. It is here that extracts can be especially valuable.

A more complete rationale for film study, practical teaching approaches, and suggestions for a film budget may be found in my *Film in the Classroom: Why Use It? How to Use It* (Dayton: Pflaum, 1971). Other materials which may be helpful in these teaching areas are:

Arnheim, Rudolf. *Visual Thinking.* Berkeley: University of California Press, 1969. $11.50.

Carrico, J. Paul. "Matter and Meaning of Motion Pictures." *English Journal* (January, 1967).

Coynik, Dave. *Film: Real to Reel.* Winona, Minnesota: St. Mary's College Press. $3.60.

Goldman, Frederick, and Linda R. Burnett. *Need Johnny Read?* Dayton: Pflaum, 1971.

Katz, John Stuart, ed. *Perspectives on the Study of Film.* Boston: Little, Brown & Co., 1971.

Lacey, Richard. *Seeing with Feeling.* Philadelphia: W. B. Saunders Co., 1972.

Laybourne, Kit, ed. *Doing the Media.* New York: The Center for Understanding Media, Inc. (75 Horatio Street, New York, New York 10014).

Maynard, Richard A. *The Celluloid Curriculum.* New York: Hayden Book Co., 1971. $7.95.

O'Grady, Gerald. "The Preparation of Teachers of Media." *Journal*

Rationale for Film Study

of Aesthetic Education (July, 1969). Urbana: University of Illinois Press. $2.25.

Peters, J.M.J. *Teaching About the Film.* New York: UNESCO, 1961.

Petric, Vladimir. "Film in the Battle of Ideas." *Art in Society,* Vol. 10, No. 2 (Summer/Fall, 1973). $2.50.

Poteet, G. Howard, ed. *The Compleat Guide to Film Study.* Urbana, Illinois: National Council of Teachers of English (NCTE), 1972. $4.75.

Schillaci, Anthony, and John Culkin, eds. *Films Deliver.* New York: Citation Press, 1970. $5.25.

Sheratsky, Rodney E. *Film: The Reality of Being.* Urbana: NCTE (1111 Kenyon Road, Urbana, Illinois 61801). $1.00.

Sohn, David. *Film Study and the English Teacher.* Bloomington: Indiana University A. V. Center. Free.

Stewart, David. *Film Study in Higher Education.* Washington, D.C.: American Council on Education, 1966. $2.75.

Sullivan, Sister Bede. *Movies: The Universal Language.* South Bend, Indiana: Fides Press, 1967. $2.45.

"The Teaching of Film." *Journal of Aesthetic Education,* Vol. 5, No. 2 (April, 1971). Urbana: University of Illinois Press. $2.25.

The Uses of Film in the Teaching of English. Ontario, Canada: Ontario Institute for Studies in Education, 1971. (Available from NCTE, $3.75.)

Chapter Three

Background on Extracts

Numerous attempts have been made by various groups of film educators and distributors to use parts of feature films in the classroom. A selective listing of these types of films—often described as extracts, excerpts, clips, or compilation films—follows, with some comments (all are available in the United States except those from the British Film Institute; a list of distributors may be found in Appendix III).

Teaching Film Custodians
Teaching Film Custodians, Inc. (TFC) has a series of abridged and edited versions of feature films, most of which are based on literary classics. These films, which generally have a running time of about 20 minutes, are intended primarily as an aid for students in literature classes; too often, however, they stress plot, dialogue, and didacticism, while shying away from the visual form and artfulness of the film. A recent production, *The American Film* (37 min.), attempts to illustrate the art of such directors as Fred Zinnemann *(High Noon)*, Alfred Hitchcock *(North by Northwest)*, William Wyler *(Friendly Persuasion)*, Elia Kazan *(On the Waterfront)*, and George Stevens *(Shane)*. Most of the TFC study guides are prepared by teachers from the National Council of Teachers of English.

British Film Institute

The approach in England is somewhat different. Years ago, the British Film Institute began using film excerpts for the serious study of film. The Institute has tried several ways of selecting its excerpts. In the first series, entitled "The Critic and Film," a film-maker, scholar, or critic described a particular shot, scene, or sequence once or several times, using an explicit script, graphs, and outlines to illustrate specific aspects of film structure and art: camera angle, lighting, editing, sound, writing, and characterization. Four films were selected for this series: David Lean's *Great Expectations* (6 min.); Harry Watt's *The Overlanders* (15 min.); Carol Reed's *Odd Man Out* (35 min.); and Sidney Lumet's *Twelve Angry Men* (25 min.). (All of these films are available from Contemporary Films.) Presumably because these excerpts were too explicit in telling students what to see in a film instead of allowing them to discover it for themselves, the Institute dropped this series and developed a second approach, which is still in operation.

For the second series, the BFI selected more than 200 extracts which are organic, unabridged, unedited, and capable of standing on their own. The selections reflect *auteur* and genre approaches to film study as well as thematic, historical, formalistic, functional, technical, national, humanistic, and social approaches. They include extracts (which run between two and twenty minutes) from the films of Welles, Kurosawa, Buñuel, Eisenstein, Vigo, Renoir, Lean, Flaherty, Huston, Wajda, Antonioni, Preminger, Fellini, Kubrick, Hawks, Bergman, Griffith, Richardson, and Truffaut; and cover comedy, Westerns, musicals, gangsters, war, the stars, heroes, love, and youth.

Originally, the only study material prepared for this series included a synopsis of both the feature and the extract, a list of cast and credits, and the film's running time. More recently, the BFI's catalog supplement includes a brief statement as to why this particular extract was selected; in some cases, information on the production crew (the actors, director, writer) and suggested teaching uses are also included. Some of the Institute's film study packages also contain a copy of the script, the source of the film (*e.g.*, a play), a tape, slides and detailed notes on both the extract and the feature.

Two different critical/educational positions have influenced the selection of these extracts. The first position, basing its ideas on those of Eisenstein, stresses (in short extracts) film language analysis; the second (in longer extracts) uses interpretative analysis to find the nature of the values the films express. Both positions concern themselves at some point with the psychological and social effects of the films on their audience.

The BFI publishes two catalogs: *Study Extract Catalogue* and its *Supplement*. While the extracts themselves are not available in the United States, the catalogs—which are an excellent resource for film teachers—are available from the BFI (see Appendix III).

The advantages of such a series are obvious: the wide variety of choice, the multiplicity of uses, the organic unity of the selection, the reliance on the extract to "speak-show" for itself, and the lack of dogmatic-literary study guides all enhance the opportunity for the teacher to use the materials well.

Other Sources of Film Extracts

Other types of films using excerpts abound, and some of the more popular and practical are:

● *The Jazz Singer* (1927), excerpts of two scenes which stress the importance of sound in the film industry (available from the Museum of Modern Art).

● Seven other excerpts from early musicals also are available from the Museum of Modern Art (MMA): *Rio Rita* (1929), *42nd Street* (1933), *Gold Diggers of 1933* and *1935, In Caliente* (1935), *Flying Down to Rio* (1933) and *Music in the Air* (1934).

● In comedy, several notable examples of excerpts are:

W. C. Fields in "Hurry Hurry" (10 min.) from *Never Give A Sucker an Even Break* and "The Great Chase" (10 min.) from *The Bank Dick.*

The Golden Age of Comedy (85 min.), with varying excerpts of Laurel and Hardy, Will Rogers, Jean Harlow, Ben Turpin, Harry Langdon; and its sequel, *When Comedy Was King* (81 min.), with Charlie Chaplin, Buster Keaton, Fatty Arbuckle, the Keystone Kops, Edgar Kennedy, and Chester Conklin. (All of the above are available from Contemporary Films.)

● Six films which deal with the work of a specific director use excerpts from each man's films:

Directed by John Ford (102 min.; FI[1]) is directed by Peter Bogdanovich and narrated by Orson Welles. One section traces American history as interpreted by excerpts from Ford's *The Iron Horse, Fort Apache, She Wore a Yellow Ribbon, The Grapes of Wrath, Cheyenne Autumn,* and 22 other films.

David Lean: A Self-Portrait (60 min.; PYR) contains excerpts from Lean's *In Which We Serve, Brief Encounter, Great Expecta-*

---

[1]A complete identification of film distributors, as well as the address of each, is listed in Appendix III.

Background on Extracts

The difficulties of growing old create conflicts between generations in *I Never Sang for My Father* with Gene Hackman (left) and Melvyn Douglas. (Columbia Pictures 1970. Screenplay by Robert Anderson, based on his play. Directed by Gilbert Cates. Excerpt: "When Parents Grow Old" LCA)

tions, *Oliver Twist, Breaking the Sound Barrier, Summertime/ Summer Madness, Dr. Zhivago, Ryan's Daughter, The Bridge on the River Kwai,* and *Lawrence of Arabia.*

Ingmar Bergman (50 min.; FI) includes clips from *Persona* and *The Touch,* along with interviews with Bergman himself, Bibi Andersson, and Max von Sydow.

Arthur Penn (1922–   ) Themes and Variants (86 min.; TWY) uses clips from *Little Big Man, Mickey One,* and others.

Arthur Penn-Little Big Man (T-L) contains interviews with Dustin Hoffman and excerpts from the feature film.

A rather interesting behind-the-scenes film entitled *The Making of Butch Cassidy and the Sundance Kid* (52 min.; A-B) contains interviews with director George Roy Hill and actors Paul Newman and Robert Redford, along with excerpts from the film.

● Numerous fine films use excerpts to document the history of films:

Hollywood: The Dream Factory (52 min.; FI) illustrates the rise and fall of the studio system by using clips from many of Hollywood's best films.

Film Firsts (2 parts, 27 min. each; ST) is a survey of early film history, from 1902 on, using clips from films by Edwin S. Porter, Georges Méliès, Thomas Ince, and D. W. Griffith.

Film and Reality (105 min.; C), compiled by Alberto Cavalcanti and Ernest Lindgren, consists of 58 documentary selections from such films as *Nanook of the North, Grass, Man of Aran, Song of Ceylon, Night Mail, The Plow That Broke the Plains,* and many others.

Neo-Realism (30 min.; TEX) documents the rise and philosophy of the Italian film movement through excerpts from *Open City, Umberto D,* and *Paisan.*

Movies Learn to Talk (26 min.; C) traces the history of film reproduction techniques from the Edison Kinetoscope to the present; it includes footage of 34 personalities and excerpts from 12 silent and sound films, including *Cyrano de Bergerac,* 1902; Barrymore's *Don Juan,* 1927; and the *Gold Diggers* musicals.

Legend of Valentino (55 min.; ST) is a biography of Rudolph Valentino with clips from *Blood and Sand* and *The Sheik.*

John Barrymore (26 min.; ST) is a biography valuable both for its story of the actor's life and its clips from many of his films.

Marilyn (83 min.; FI) features Rock Hudson narrating the career of M.M. with excerpts from *Gentlemen Prefer Blondes, Monkey Business, Niagara, Bus Stop,* and others.

The Legend of Marilyn Monroe (60 min.; MPC), Terry Sanders' recapitulation of Monroe's life, features clips from her famous films; this film was produced by David Wolper.

Hollywood: The Golden Years (60 min.; MPC), narrated by a good-humored Gene Kelly, is the first of the Hollywood compilations produced by David Wolper.

Hollywood: The Fabulous Era (60 min.; MPC), narrated by Henry Fonda, contains clips featuring such actors as Bette Davis, Judy Garland, Errol Flynn, and James Cagney.

Hollywood: The Great Stars (60 min.; MPC) includes films of the great studios—MGM, Paramount, Warner, United Artists—and some of their equally great stars.

A Tribute to Warner Brothers (90 min.; WB) is a compliment to a studio, its directors and stars; its excerpts include scenes from *Little Caesar, Public Enemy, I Am a Fugitive from a Chain Gang, The Sea Hawk,* and many others.

Many film distributors carry compilation reels of early silent films. For example, the Kemp Niver series on the very early history of film is distributed by Pyramid under the title *The First Twenty Years* and by Macmillan/Audio-Brandon as *In The Beginning.* Other reels stressing the beginnings of film (*Archaeology of the Cinema, The Great Chase, The Eternal Tramp,* etc.) may be found by checking the catalogs of Creative Film Society, Em Gee, and Willoughby-Peerless.

● Some film excerpts exist primarily for the study of film techniques and style. A few of the best are as follows:

Hollywood Magic Camp (45 min.; CFS) consists of several sequences from films of the Thirties that use special effects, including *King Kong* and Busby Berkeley films.

The Birth of a Nation, "The Homecoming Scene" (4 min.; MMA)—the "Little Colonel" returns to his war-ravaged home, a classic example of camera placement, editing, and acting.

The Battleship Potemkin, "The Odessa Steps" sequence (10 min.; MMA)—the supreme example of Eisenstein's concept of montage.

Olympiad, "The Diving Sequence" (5 min.; MMA)—Leni Riefenstahl's example of editing time and space from concrete to abstract to beauty.

Olympiad, "Marathon" sequence (13 min.; Image Resources)—brilliant camera work and editing follow Japan's Kitei San to his triumph in the 26-mile marathon in the 1936 Olympics.

The Eye Hears, the Ear Sees (58 min.; IFB) includes excerpts from *Neighbors* and all of *Pas de Deux* in order to illustrate Canadian National Film Board's Norman McLaren's inventive animation techniques.

Western Hero (26 min.; UCE)—a brief historical survey of Western film heroes featuring excerpts from *The Iron Horse, Stagecoach,* and *High Noon.*

The Art of the Impossible (27 min.; LCA) uses clips from *The Birth of a Nation, The Battleship Potemkin, Footlight Parade, King Kong, Lawrence of Arabia, The African Queen,* and *Downhill Racer* to illustrate film's ability to create reality out of illusion.

Learning Corporation of America

One of the most recent uses of the excerpt idea is a series of 15 films, distributed by Learning Corporation of America (LCA), entitled "Searching for Values: A Film Anthology." These films (all produced by Columbia Pictures) have been cut in one of two ways: either in single sequences with little editing, as in the BFI approach, or in abridgements with considerable editing of the narrative. The films run 15 to 17 minutes apiece; entirely content-oriented, they deal with such basic issues as responsibility, ethics, violence, racism, goals in life, and love. The films are intended for use in the classroom (English, social studies, humanities, religion, and psychology). A few of the better titles, with their sources, are:

"The Dehumanizing City," from *Tiger Makes Out;*
"My Country Right or Wrong," from *I Never Sang for My Father;*
"Love and Loneliness," from *Five Easy Pieces;*
"The Right to Live," from *Abandon Ship;*
"Friendship or Conscience," from *On the Waterfront.*

Film Extracts on Television

Recent uses of extracts from feature films may be found on two programs on educational television, and eventually may be available for classroom use. One, *The Movie World of Ingmar Bergman,* produced by David Wilson, presents 20 feature films directed by the great Swedish artist, each of which is introduced by Chicago *Sun-Times* film critic Roger Ebert. Ebert selected four or five extracts from Bergman's films to illustrate the director's use of certain themes, his stock company of actors, and his visual style. Thematically, the films (supported by extracts of five to ten minutes) trace such consistent ideas as the silence of God, the difficulty of communication between people, and the artist's suffering during the creative act. Stylistically, the extracts cover recurring images of clocks and mirrors, Bergman's use of journeys, and

A young man (Jack Nicholson) is confused about choices in his life in *Five Easy Pieces*. (Columbia Pictures 1970. Directed by Bob Rafelson. Excerpt: "Loneliness and Loving" LCA)

silence. These films were shown in 1973 and 1974 on Chicago's local television station, WTTW/Channel 11. Further information about their availability may be obtained from WTTW, Educational Services Division, 5400 North St. Louis Ave., Chicago, Illinois 60625; phone (312) 583-5000.

A second program, *Men Who Made the Movies,* uses interviews with seven American directors and extracts from their feature films to highlight both the history of film and the career of film artists in Hollywood. The directors include Raoul Walsh, Frank Capra, Howard Hawks, King Vidor, Alfred Hitchcock, Vincente Minnelli, and William Wellman. During the program the last director, for example, discusses selections from his films: *Wings, Public Enemy, Wild Boys, A Star Is Born, Buffalo Bill, The Story of G. I. Joe,* and *The Ox-Bow Incident.* The series was produced, directed, and written by film critic Richard Schickel, narrated by Cliff Robertson, and sponsored by the Eastman Kodak Company; it was shown on the national educational television network. Further information may be obtained from the Eastman Kodak Company or from WNET, 304 West 58th Street, New York, New York 10019.

Chapter Four

Rationale for the Use of Extracts

Obviously, the increasing use of film excerpts is based on some kind of rationale. For the most part, extracts are convenient and relatively inexpensive for the film teacher to rent or buy. While no serious film teacher believes that extracts are the only answer to such problems in film teaching as limited budgets, 50-minute class periods, appropriateness, availability, and selectivity of film materials, extracts *can* be an additional tool for the teacher. The use of extracts, as well as the kind of extracts selected, will vary with the nature of the course, the talent of the teacher, the amount of the budget, and the size and ability of the classes themselves.

Basically, the ways to use extracts are simple:

1. Extract alone—to anchor discussion solidly to what actually occurred on the screen;

2. Extract with other extracts—for comparison and contrast;

3. Extract with the same full-length feature—as a "memory trigger" to initiate and stimulate discussion or to zero-in on specific issues or elements of the film;

4. Extract with other features;

5. Extract with other non-film materials (short stories, plays, novels, scripts, sound tracks on record or tape, stills, posters, slides, and filmstrips).

An elaboration of these uses is in order. In my experience, I have found extracts most useful when they are used along with a feature film and other materials over a period of several weeks. Whether the extract is used by itself or with other materials, its important use is in detailed, comprehensive film analysis. Usually, a feature film is booked for one showing on one day or in a series in which each reel is shown once over a period of several days, and then the film must be returned to the distributor. In order to be quite specific in discussing a particular sequence, the teacher can show the extract once or more after the feature itself has been returned. Just as individual words, lines, stanzas, scenes, and chapters can be singled out for concentrated and extended study in literature, so also can shots, scenes, situations, and sequences from film be used in a worthwhile manner for in-depth study—not only of content but of form, which always implies the artful selection and arrangement of content. This technique is similar in practice to the approach of the "New Critics" in literature (John Crowe Ransom, Allen Tate, Robert Penn Warren, and Cleanth Brooks) which has fostered close reading of the literary text.

With one extract of approximately 15 minutes, which is usually about one-eighth the length of a feature film, the teacher can limit his objectives; thus, the student can concentrate on fewer objectives and be better able to accomplish them. A thorough study of Welles' *Citizen Kane* or Ford's *The Grapes of Wrath* is most difficult for high school students because of the myriad possibilities of approach; but with an extract of the "breakfast scene" with Kane and his first wife, Emily, or the "bulldozer scene" with Muley squatting over "his" dusty farm from *The Grapes of Wrath*, the students and teacher can focus their attention specifically on any one element of editing, sound, acting, camera placement, composition, lighting, style, flashbacks, point of view, major and minor themes. With this select and concentrated type of viewing, the student then has an opportunity to articulate his own experience in sharp detail, whether in discussion or in writing.

The range of extract use is wide; potentially, it can accommodate most approaches of film teachers and film curricula: the study of authorship, film history, film style and technique, themes, and genre. The examples which follow are based on some extracts that have been made by the British Film Institute (but which are unavailable in the United States) and others which are possibilities for future projects. Of course, the film study approaches that will be discussed also could be done with the complete features, if the teacher's budget and time schedule allow.

The Study of Authorship

Most often, authorship study means a study of the director, although it need not be limited to such a narrow interpretation. In a study of John Ford, for example, the teacher might show the feature film *Stagecoach* as a central work of Ford, then use the excerpt from *My Darling Clementine*, or the full-length feature *The Iron Horse* or *The Man Who Shot Liberty Valance* to illustrate the development of this artist. Or, as Andrew Sarris suggests in *The American Cinema*, one could study the works *(oeuvres)* of Orson Welles, through his features and extracts, from the "psychological density of the fictionalized biography *(Citizen Kane)* and filmed novel *(The Magnificent Ambersons)* to the psychological abstractions of fantasy *(The Lady from Shanghai)*, allegory *(Touch of Evil)*, fable *(Mr. Arkadin)*, hallucination *(The Trial)*, and reverie *(Falstaff)*."[1] (Possible extracts from *Citizen Kane* are now being considered by Films Incorporated.) Again, a course on Hitchcock or the thriller might use the features *Psycho* and *Vertigo* and support these with excerpts from *The 39 Steps* (as an example of Hitchcock's early British work) and *North by Northwest* (as an example of his American light-comedy style).

While using excerpts to study the style of a director is one logical approach to authorship study, excerpts also can be used to study the versatile contributions of actors, writers, cinematographers, composers and, even, the studios. In regard to acting, for example, one might compare the early James Cagney as a gangster in *Public Enemy* (1931) or dancer in *Footlight Parade* (1933) with the later Cagney in *White Heat* (1949) or *Yankee Doodle Dandy* (1942). Excerpts would be helpful for a study of the development of an actor under the same director. John Ford, who directed Henry Fonda in *The Grapes of Wrath* (1940), *My Darling Clementine* (1946), and *Fort Apache* (1948); or John Huston, who used Humphrey Bogart in *The Maltese Falcon* (1941), *The Treasure of the Sierra Madre* (1947), and *The African Queen* (1951).

As for the writer's contribution, a sample package of the following might be worthwhile: the script *Stagecoach*, by John Ford and Dudley Nichols (available from Simon and Schuster, New York), which includes the short story *Stage to Lordsburg*, by Ernest Haycox, as well as the original adaptation by Dudley Nichols and the changes which were made in the final version of the film; the feature film *Stagecoach* (1939) itself; and a film extract, either of the two towns or of the Indian chase. Or, again using writer Dudley Nichols as an example, an interesting lesson might be to compare a chapter from Liam O'Flaherty's novel, *The Informer*, with the same scene as it was interpreted by Nichols (who won an

[1]Andrew Sarris, *The American Cinema: Directors and Directions 1929-1968* (New York: Dutton, 1968), p. 78.

Rationale for Extracts   21

Academy Award for the script of *The Informer*) and Ford in the film: the trial of Gypo, for example, or his death.

One also could choose the play *The Front Page* (1928), By Ben Hecht and Charles MacArthur, and compare the changes made by the screenwriters and directors in the two film versions—*The Front Page* (1931), directed by Lewis Milestone with the scenario by Bartlett Cormack and Charles Lederer, and *His Girl Friday* (1940), directed by Howard Hawks and scripted by Charles Lederer. Extracts could be used to center on how the main character, reporter Hildy Johnson, is introduced and developed, or on one confrontation of Hildy—played by Pat O'Brien in the earlier film and Rosalind Russell in the later one—with the publisher of the paper, Walter Burns (played by Adolphe Menjou in the earlier film and Cary Grant in the later version). This particular unit was taught by Professor Stuart Kaminsky in a 1973 film workshop, "The Screen Arts and the American Educational Experience," at the University of Illinois circle campus in Chicago, sponsored by the Screen Educators' Society.

A Selected Bibliography

Four books which are quite constructive in creating a lesson or course on "The Writer as Auteur" and in studying the contributions and problems of the screenwriter are:

Corliss, Richard, ed. *The Hollywood Screenwriters.* New York: Avon Books, 1970.
Froug, William. *The Screenwriter Looks at the Screenwriter.* New York: Macmillan, 1972.
McCarty, Clifford. *Published Screenplays: A Checklist.* Kent, Ohio: Kent State University Press, 1971.
Trumbo, Dalton. *Additional Dialogue.* New York: Bantam Books, 1972.

Specific short extracts are of exceptional value in the study of the craft of cinematographers and musical composers, who are seldom mentioned either in writing or in film courses. The director of photography is responsible for the visual style of the film, as opposed to its content, as requested by or worked out cooperatively with the director. The muscial composer may work with the director as the film is being shot or, more usually, after the film is completed. One could select scenes from the work of Gregg Toland in Welles' *Citizen Kane* and in Ford's *The Grapes of Wrath;* or of James Wong Howe in Martin Ritt's *Hud* and in Frank-

A sailor (Tyrone Power) must make vital decisions about who shall survive in *Abandon Ship*. (Columbia Pictures 1957. Directed by Richard Sale. Excerpt: "Right to Live" LCA)

enheimer's *Seconds;* or of Sven Nykvist in Bergman's *The Virgin Spring, The Silence,* or *The Passion of Anna* and in Conrad Rooks' *Siddhartha;* or of Lucien Ballard in Peckinpah's *The Wild Bunch* and in Tom Gries' *Will Penny.*

For too long a time have brilliant cinematographers been neglected. (John Simon is one of the very few critics who regularly acknowledge the expert contributions of cinematographers.) These artists are people like William Daniels *(Brute Force, The Naked City),* Stanley Cortez *(The Magnificent Ambersons, Night of the Hunter),* Lee Garmes *(Shanghai Express, Scarface),* Haskell Wexler *(America, America; Who's Afraid of Virginia Woolf?),* Sol Polito *(Sorry, Wrong Number; The Sea Hawk),* and Vilmos Zsigmond *(McCabe and Mrs. Miller, The Hired Hand).*

A Selected Bibliography

Three helpful resources for teaching a unit on directors of photography are:

"Great Cameramen." *Focus on Film,* No. 13. London: Tantivy Press (108 New Bond Street, London, England W1Y OQX). 84 pp.

Higham, Charles. *Hollywood Cameramen: Sources of Light.* Bloomington: Indiana University Press, 1970.

Koszarski, Richard, compiler. "60 Filmographies: The Men with the Movie Cameras." *Film Comment* (Summer, 1972), pp. 27–57.

In regard to studying the work of musical composers, the teacher will find that extracts can be most helpful, for audiences seldom consciously recognize a film's musical background. The value of an extract in this case is that it can be shown several times in one class period, with or without the sound. For example, the class might view the opening sequence of Frankenheimer's *Seconds,* in which William Randolph walks through Grand Central Station and is handed a note. The extract can be shown with the sound track and without it, but the viewer immediately realizes that the function of the music by Jerry Goldsmith is to set the entire tone of impending horror in the film. Or one can pay special attention to comparing the works of such composers as Alfred Newman in *The Grapes of Wrath* and *My Darling Clementine;* or Max Steiner in *King Kong* and *The Treasure of the Sierra Madre;* or Dmitri Tiomkin in *High Noon* and *Red River;* or Nino Rota in *La Strada* and *The Godfather;* or Bernard Herrmann in *Citizen Kane, Psycho,* and *The Day the Earth Stood Still.*

In my own classes I have tried a variation of the extract approach: over a two-semester film course I taped ten 30-second pieces of musical background from various films (*e.g.*, the poignant violins which played as Antoine Doinel ran toward the sea in the last sequence of *The 400 Blows;* from *Dr. Strangelove,* "Try a Little Tenderness" [as the B-52 refueled in the air] and "We'll Meet Again" [during the scene of the destruction of the Earth]; the idealistic song "Even the Horses Have Wings," from *Taking Off,* which played while the parents and neighbors visited the daughter's room; the title song which accompanied a love scene from *Elvira Madigan;* the solemn but humorous funeral march from *Divorce Italian Style;* the tense opening and closing music from *Seconds;* the musical background for the haunting scenes of atomic destruction in *La Jetée;* and the grim music which played during the opening travel shots of the camps in *Night and Fog*). At the end of the course I replayed each selection and discussed such aspects as how the music created a mood, how it reinforced the visual situation, and its overall effectiveness.

Selected Records

A number of record albums are available to enhance this type of lesson:

Music from Great Film Classics (SP-44144, London), conducted by composer Bernard Herrmann, contains music from *Citizen Kane, Jane Eyre, The Snows of Kilimanjaro.*

Music from the Great Movie Thrillers (SP-44126, London), conducted by Bernard Herrmann, contains scores from director Alfred Hitchcock's *Psycho, Marnie, North by Northwest, Vertigo.*

Now Voyager: The Classic Film Scores of Max Steiner (ARL 1-0136, RCA) contains scores from *King Kong, The Big Sleep, The Informer,* and others.

The Sea Hawk: The Classic Film Scores of Erich Wolfgang Korngold (LSC-3330, RCA) contains scores from *Robin Hood, Of Human Bondage, Captain Blood.*

Starring Fred Astaire (Columbia Records SG 32472) includes 31 recordings from 1935–38; songs and dances from *Top Hat, Follow the Fleet, Swing Time, Shall We Dance, A Damsel in Distress,* and *Carefree.*

Film History

A great variety of possibilities for the use of extracts exists in this area. A study of the development of the American film as narrative art could use a full-length feature of D. W. Griffith *(Intolerance, The Birth of a Nation, Broken Blossoms)*, for example, supported by extracts from a film of Orson Welles or John Huston. A study of the important developments in the national cinemas of Russia, Italy, or France might be achieved by contrasting a feature film from one major director with extracts by other directors. For example, the early use of film editing can be compared in extracts from Eisenstein's *The Battleship Potemkin* and sections from Pudovkin's *Mother* and Dovzhenko's *Earth;* the development of Neo-Realism, through extracts of Rossellini's *Open City* and a feature such as de Sica's *Bicycle Thieves* or Fellini's *La Strada;* the thrust of the New Wave, in extracts and features of Truffaut *(The 400 Blows)*, Godard *(Breathless)*, Malle *(The Lovers)*, Resnais *(Hiroshima Mon Amour)*, Chabrol *(The Cousins)*, and Camus *(Black Orpheus)*. This type of approach to film is important in that it can analyze the individual films and extracts in themselves, chart their influence on other directors, and detail significant trends in the brief history of film.

Film Style and Technique

Again in this approach, extracts lend themselves particularly well to a wealth of teaching possibilities. *Citizen Kane* is a virtual compendium of technical gems in its use of cinematography, the use of deep focus and wide-angle lens with ceilinged sets; editing, the compact mode of narrative through flashback; and the superb use of sound which resulted from Welles' experience in both radio and the theater. Any one of the major flashbacks or the newsreel sequence would suffice adequately for intensive study. A fine comparison could be made between Gregg Toland's use of deep focus in *Citizen Kane* (1941) and James Wong Howe's use of wide-angle lens, deep focus, and claustrophobic sets inside a ship in William K. Howard's *Transatlantic,* made 10 years earlier. Another comparison might be of a film's narrative structures, especially between the flashbacks in *Citizen Kane* (written by Welles and Herman Mankiewicz) and Howard's *The Power and the Glory* (1933), written by Preston Sturges.

In a discussion of the different uses of editing, an extract of "The Odessa Steps" from *The Battleship Potemkin* or the "shower murder" from Hitchcock's *Psycho* could stand as a classic example of montage and shock cutting; excerpts from Don Siegel's *Baby Face Nelson* and William Wyler's *The Best Years of Our Lives* are fine examples of functional, or invisible, editing; and excerpts from Renoir's *Rules of the Game* and Bertolucci's *The Conformist* serve as examples of camera movement substituting for cutting.

Other carefully selected extracts could be used to illustrate the expressive use of sound in films: *e.g.,* the tragic crowing of Emil Jannings in Von Sternberg's *The Blue Angel;* the sultry singing of the dance-hall girl, Ivy, in Rouben Mamoulian's *Dr. Jekyll and Mr. Hyde;* and Peter Lorre's ominous whistling of the refrain from Grieg's *Peer Gynt Suite* in Fritz Lang's *M.* Specific scenes from Robert Wiene's *The Cabinet of Dr. Caligari,* Eisenstein's *Ivan the Terrible,* and Wilder's *Sunset Boulevard* could be used to emphasize the importance of costume, decor, and set design in achieving the total powerful effects of these films. Brief extracts could be used to study the development, function, and artistry of color in such films as D. W. Griffith's *The Birth of a Nation* (a number of frames were tinted by hand), Mamoulian's *Becky Sharp,* Victor Fleming's *The Wizard of Oz,* Michelangelo Antonioni's *The Red Desert,* Bertolucci's *The Conformist,* Jan Troell's *The Emigrants,* Jerry Lewis' *The Family Jewels,* or Alfred Hitchcock's *Marnie.*

A fascinating course in "film noir" could use extracts to intensify the theme of post-war cynicism through an analysis of such stylistic film elements as dark lighting of both sets and actors; oblique lines and chaotic compositions; actual locales of streets, alleys, and docks; and disorienting flashbacks in films like Edward Dmytryk's *Murder My Sweet,* Welles' *The Lady from Shanghai,* Billy Wilder's *Double Indemnity,* Lang's *The Big Heat,* Robert Aldrich's *Kiss Me Deadly,* Robert Siodmak's *Cry of the City,* and Raoul Walsh's *White Heat.*

Film Themes

Many courses and units in English, the humanities, social studies, philosophy, and cinema are constructed around a theme or themes. Of numerous themes, some of the more popular are war, violence, youth, the hero, love, the city, institutions, prejudice, the individual/loner, social problems, values, and women. A study of the treatment of youth might use a full-length feature, such as *The 400 Blows,* with excerpts from Mike Nichols' *The Graduate,* Roeg's *Walkabout,* Don Owen's *Nobody Waved Goodbye,* Vigo's *Zéro de Conduite,* Lindsay Anderson's *If . . . ,* Peter Bogdanovich's *Paper Moon,* Ermanno Olmi's *Il Posto,* and Peter Brooks' *Lord of the Flies.* The treatment of war, through different national viewpoints, could be studied through extracts of Kubrick's *Paths of Glory,* Resnais' *Hiroshima Mon Amour,* Wajda's *Kanal,* Ichikawa's *Fires on the Plain,* Rossellini's *Paisa,* Chukrai's *Ballad of a Soldier,* Milestone's *Pork Chop Hill,* Cornel Wilde's *Beach Red,* Siegel's *Hell Is for Heroes,* and Fuller's *The Steel Helmet.* Excerpts also could be used in a study of the treatment of racial themes and stereotypes in such films as Vincente Minnelli's *Cabin in the Sky,* William Keighley's *Green Pastures,* Archie Mayo's *Black Legion,* Dmytryk's *Crossfire,* and Kadar's *Shop on Main Street.* Changes in the filmic treatment of blacks could be documented through extracts of Stepin Fetchit in John Ford's *Steamboat Round the Bend* (1935) and Richard Roundtree in Gordon Parks' *Shaft.*

A Selected Bibliography
Several resources for developing a thematic approach are:

British Film Institute. "Some Suggested Themes and Materials." London: Education Department, B.F.I. (81 Dean St., London, England W1V 6AA).

Feyen, Sharon, and Donald Wigal, eds. *Screen Experience: An Approach to Film.* Dayton: Pflaum, 1969.

Hall, Stuart, and Paddy Whannel. *The Popular Arts.* New York: Pantheon, 1965.

Lacey, Richard A. *Seeing with Feeling: Film in the Classroom.* Philadelphia: W. B. Saunders Co., 1972.

Mallery, David. *The School and the Art of Motion Pictures.* Boston: National Association of Independent Schools (4 Liberty Square, Boston, Massachusetts 02109), 1966.

Maynard, Richard. *The Celluloid Curriculum.* New York: Hayden Book Co., 1971.

Film Genre
Some teachers arrange their film courses and units with a concern for the Hollywood genre film. Since the extracts discussed later in this book have been selected primarily on the basis of a genre approach, some notes are necessary about the place of genre in the study of film.

Attempting a definition of *genre* is both easy and difficult. Simply, it means "kind, sort, or type," and is derived from the Latin root "genus." Originally the term was used, as it still is, to classify literature and literary history—not by time or place, but by literary types of organization and structure. Although Aristotle, in his *Poetics,* distinguished among literary types such as tragedy, epic, and lyric, the term came into more general use in the 17th and 18th centuries, with specific differentiation made among such forms as pastoral, elegy, ode, epic, tragedy, satire, and comedy. The 19th century saw the continued use of the term, particularly in the development of the novel, in such sub-genres as the historical, political, and Gothic novels.

The literary functions of genre, which were concisely articulated by the 19th century Romantic poet Samuel Taylor Coleridge, in his *Biographia Literaria*, apply equally well to film genre. Coleridge discusses the principles of recognition and surprise in genre: the recurrence of thematic statement, image, sounds, or symbols is pleasurable for the reader whenever he discovers a new instance of a motif; or when the reader recognizes motifs, themes, or elements in different manifestations, his pleasurable recognition is augmented and enhanced by pleasurable perception of the difference. According to Rene Wellek and Austin Warren, in *Theory of Literature*, genre may be based on "outer form (specific meter or structure) and inner form (attitude, tone, purpose—more crudely, subject and audience)." [2]

The application of genre in the study of film has significance because film, as a popular and high art form, can reveal many details about a particular culture—its people, its art, its manner of communication—as well as the basics of human perception of life, through such universal elements as man's hopes, fears, dreams, and values. Genre study in film involves the analysis of certain common ideas, themes, and motifs, typical actions and situations, expressed by characters with a cluster of recognizable attributes, in a previously defined setting, all of which are synthesized by a narrative or dramatic structure. This structure is composed of both the old and the new—what John Cawelti, in *The Six-Gun Mystique*, calls "conventions and inventions" [3]: the former, familiar and shared images and meanings which assert on-going continuity of values; the latter, new and unrealized perceptions or meanings. The degree of pleasure the audience derives from a genre film depends on the filmmaker's artistic blending of a sense of novelty with a sense of recognition. The genre represents a total of aesthetic devices accessible to the filmmaker and understandable to his audience. The filmmaker can manipulate these conventions by conforming to them or expanding them.

The conventional element of the gun battle in the Western, for example, requires two men to use guns and confront one another. In Henry King's *The Gunfighter*, however, Gregory Peck (as Jimmy Ringo) defeats his opponent, Skip Homeier, in a duel situation without ever having to use a gun. Instead, he uses the threat of a gun hidden under a table to bluff his antagonist. Thus, King

[2] Rene Wellek and Austin Warren, *Theory of Literature* (New York: Harcourt, Brace, 1956), p. 221.

[3] John Cawelti, *The Six-Gun Mystique* (Bowling Green, Ohio: Bowling Green University Popular Press, 1970), p. 28.

Rationale for Extracts

conforms to the convention of using a gun battle but inventively stretches the convention by having not one shot fired or one person killed.

The elements of convention often are made up of myths—universal demonstrations of inner meaning from what Carl Jung calls "the collective unconscious" and Claude Lévi-Strauss describes as expressions of unobservable realities in terms of observable phenomena. By "myth" is meant not fallacious history, but a body of tradition about the past—a kind of collective dream. The myths serve as media through which archetypes (universal symbols, motifs, heroes, patterns) become understandable to man's consciousness. Both the myth and the archetype can be expressed in formula, or genre, the functions of which are to pinpoint and reinforce the values of a particular society, to provide a continual link between old and new cultures, and to become a model for the creation of artistic work. As a concise shorthand to man's being, myths attempt to represent reality and universal patterns of experience—whether of man's birth, growth, or death.

Each culture develops its own genres to express myths and archetypes. In a study of American genre films, certain characters can be analyzed as they work out their film roles to fulfill both the narrative of the film and the larger aspects of the "American dream," or myth.

The Gunfighter, for example, plays on a twist of the archetypes of initiation and the scapegoat: not only is Jimmy Ringo's desire to be reunited with his family shattered, but he must undergo a series of painful physical and psychological ordeals as he tries to return from "experience" (his days of killing) to "innocence" (with his wife and son); in addition, he must die in order to atone for his misdeeds (and those of other gunfighters), even though he may have killed in self-defense. The "American dream" concept, or myth, of a new "Adam" in the Garden of Eden is tragically tarnished by this hero who is no longer innocent, pure, or uncompromised.

In viewing a genre film, the audience has a preconceived set of expectations to be fulfilled; yet this unwritten code between the filmmaker and his audience consists of no rigid or fixed ideal form. It has developed, not through one film or one director, but over a period of years and in many films by many directors, into a flexible tradition. The genre film is made up of a number of possibilities which the filmmaker has chosen, because of his own personal vision, to fuse historical and mythical subject matter and setting, thematic concerns, individual and archetypal characters,

Rationale for Extracts

Terry Malloy (Marlon Brando) is ostracized because he stood up for justice in *On the Waterfront*. (Columbia Pictures 1954. Story and screenplay by Budd Schulberg from his novel. Directed by Elia Kazan. Excerpt: "Whether to Tell the Truth" LCA)

and iconography into a rhetorical and loose structure. The term "iconography" is one borrowed from art by Erwin Panofsky, who describes it as a "branch of art history which concerns itself with subject matter or meaning of works of art as opposed to their form." Based on a Greek word meaning "image," icons and iconography are discussed by Colin McArthur, in *Underworld U.S.A.*, in terms of patterns of recurring visual images in gangster and thriller films: the physical presences of James Cagney and Edward G. Robinson, for example—their facial expressions; their movements, speech patterns, and dress; the environment of the city, with rooming houses, bars, and alleys; and the technology of the city at the character's disposal—guns, cars, telephones.

Through the artistic treatment and style of the director, the scriptwriter, and the cinematographer, these recurring patterns of visual imagery are able to crystallize ideas for the audience, to unite the past with the present, and to express a deep sense of togetherness in feeling, action, and being. The conventional genre elements of plot, character, setting, visual patterns, and style can frame, isolate, and enhance a director's interpretation of humanity in specific situations. Although Shakespeare often dealt with familiar legends (doomed lovers in *Romeo and Juliet)* and standard patterns (revenge/tragedy in *Hamlet*), he personalized his plays with his own stamp of individual brilliance. So also have the following filmmakers used their talent, through the genre film, to make valuable artistic statements about the human condition: John Ford, in the Western; Gene Kelly, in the musical; George Pal, in science fiction; the Marx Brothers, in comedy: Roger Corman, in the gangster film; and, of course, Howard Hawks, in such genres as the gangster film *(Scarface)*, the thriller *(The Big Sleep)*, comedy *(Bringing Up Baby)*, the Western *(Red River)*, and science fiction *(The Thing)*.

Each new film in a particular genre, more so if it is a proven commercial success, increases the genre's sense of tradition. Films are influenced by films. They can imitate, parody, transform other films into unique reverberations. And now, with genre films being shown to large audiences both in theaters and on television (often in a brutally aborted form to accommodate network time schedules and commercials), and with the technology of making films more available than ever before, the genres have been forced either to expand and revitalize themselves—as have the Western (Peckinpah's *The Wild Bunch*) and the gangster film (Coppola's *The Godfather)*—or to atrophy. Spy films, for example, have virtually disappeared—or have been forced to parody themselves (as in *Goldfinger*). The fact that genre films like *The God-father* and *The Poseidon Adventure* are more regularly viewed by audiences than are high-art films (such as those of Bergman or Fellini) suggests not only the conscious desire for entertainment on the part of most viewers but also that their unconscious needs are at least appealed to, if not fulfilled, by the genre film.

Professor Stuart Kaminsky, in his book *American Film Genres*, makes a strong case for the serious study of popular genre films. He argues that if a film or genre is popular, it is responding to an interest—even a need—of its culture. Therefore, the film should be thoroughly analyzed and understood before it is evaluated or dismissed. This analysis should not limit itself only to the literary or filmic elements of the film, but should be expanded to include basic aspects of "existence and social/psychological interaction." Kaminsky also stresses that genre criticism does not seek to dogmatize but rather to recognize that a form exists which must be examined in order to see what it means and how it is used in a particular film.

An analysis of a genre film can accommodate other approaches as well: the contribution of the director, as *auteur*, to the genre (what Peckinpah adds to the Western, for example); thematic concerns (the fear of doom usually present in a science fiction film); use of film rhetoric (such as montage in a science fiction film and gangster film); function of symbols (the sexual imagery in *Dr. Strangelove*); or film history (the development of "film noir"). In fact, I have found that multiple and flexible critical approaches to the study of film are most rewarding because this blend comes closest to the total potential vision of the medium. Film is an all-encompassing medium relating to social studies, psychology, art, literature, politics, and communications. No one approach is able to fully exhaust the many interpretive possibilities of a worthwhile film. All approaches have both advantages and limitations.

Bibliography for the Study of Genre

Alloway, Lawrence. *Violent America: The Movies 1946–1964.* Greenwich, Connecticut: Museum of Modern Art, 1971.
Balázs, Béla. *Theory of the Film.* New York: Dover, 1970.
Barthes, Roland. *Mythologies.* New York: Hill and Wang, 1972.
Bayer, William. *The Great Movies.* New York: Grosset and Dunlap, 1973.
Bazin, André. *What Is Cinema?* Tr. by Hugh Gray. Vol. II. Berke-

ley: University of California Press, 1971.

Bodkin, Maud. *Archetypal Patterns in Poetry: Psychological Studies of Imagination.* New York: Oxford University Press, 1934.

_____. *Studies of Type Images in Poetry, Religion, and Philosophy.* Folcroft, Pennsylvania: Folcroft Library Editions, 1951.

Buscombe, Ed. "The Idea of Genre in American Cinema." *Screen* (March/April, 1970).

Campbell, Joseph, ed. *Myths, Dreams, and Religion.* New York: Dutton, 1970.

Cavell, Stanley. *The World Viewed.* New York: Viking Press, 1971.

Cawelti, John. "The Concept of Formula in Study of Popular Literature." *Journal of Popular Culture,* Vol. 3, No. 3. Winter, 1969.

_____. *The Six-Gun Mystique.* Bowling Green, Ohio: Bowling Green University Popular Press, 1970.

"Cinema Semiotics and the Work of Christian Metz." *Screen* (Spring/Summer, 1973).

Collins, R. "A Genre: Reply to Ed Buscombe's." *Screen* (July/October, 1970).

_____. "Mythic Knowledge and Its Mediation in the American Cinema." *Screen Education Notes,* Vol. 7 (Summer, 1973).

Frazier, James. *The New Golden Bough.* Revised and edited by T. H. Gaster. New York: Mentor, 1964.

Freud, Sigmund. *Totem and the Taboo.* New York: Vintage, 1948.

Frye, Northrop. *Anatomy of Criticism: Four Essays.* Princeton, New Jersey: Princeton University Press, 1971.

_____. *Fables of Identity: Studies in Poetic Mythology.* New York: Harcourt, Brace, 1963.

Guerin, Wilfred L., *et al. A Handbook of Critical Approaches to Literature.* New York: Harper & Row, 1966.

Hess, Judith W. "Genre Films and the Status Quo," *Jump Cut,* No. 1 (May-June, 1974) pp. 1, 16, 18.

Jung, Carl, G. Adler, *et al,* eds. *Archetypes and the Collective Unconscious.* Princeton: Princeton University Press, 1969.

Jung, Carl, ed. *Man and His Symbols.* New York: Dell, 1971.

_____. *The Portable Jung.* New York: Viking Press, 1971.

Kaminsky, Stuart. *American Film Genres.* Dayton, Ohio: Pflaum, 1974.

_____. *Myth to Screen: A Genre Anthology* (tentative title). Dayton: Pflaum, 1975.

Kitses, Jim. *Horizons West.* Bloomington: Indiana University Press, 1969.

Kracauer, Siegfried. *From Caligari to Hitler.* Princeton: Princeton University Press, 1966.

Rationale for Extracts

Leach, Ed. *Claude Lévi-Strauss.* New York: Viking Press, 1970.

Lévi-Strauss, Claude "Structural Study of Myth." *Journal of American Folklore,* LXXVIII (October/December, 1955), pp 428-444.

Lewis, R.W.B. *The American Adam.* Chicago: University of Chicago Press, 1955.

Matthews, Jack, ed. *Archetypal Themes in Modern Story.* New York: St. Martin's Press, 1973.

McArthur, Colin. "Genre and Iconography." *B.F.I. Report* (March, 1969).

————. *Underworld U.S.A.* New York: Viking Press, 1972.

Munsterberg, Hugo. *The Film: A Psychological Study.* New York: Dover, 1970.

Panofsky, Erwin. *Meaning in the Visual Arts.* Garden City, New York: Doubleday, 1955.

————. *Studies in Iconology: Humanistic Themes in the Art of the Renaissance.* New York: Harper & Row, 1972.

Philipson, Morris, ed. *Aesthetics Today.* New York: Meridian Publishers, 1971.

Rohdie, Sam. "Style, Rhetoric and Genre." *B.F.I. Report* (March, 1970).

————. "Totems and Movies." *B.F.I. Report* (January, 1969).

Ryall, Tom. "The Notion of Genre." *Screen* (March/April, 1970).

Smith, Henry Nash. *The Virgin Land: The American West as Symbol and Myth.* London: Oxford University Press, 1973. Revised edition.

Tudor, Andrew. "Genre: Theory and Mispractice in Film Criticism." *Screen* (November/December, 1970).

Tyler, Parker. *Magic and Myth in Movies.* New York: Simon and Schuster, 1970.

Wellek, Rene, and Austin Warren. *Theory of Literature.* New York: Harcourt, Brace, 1956.

Whannel, Paddy, and Stuart Hall. *The Popular Arts.* New York: Pantheon, 1965.

Wolfenstein, Martha, and Nathan Leites. *Movies: A Psychological Study.* New York: Atheneum, 1970.

Wollen, Peter. *Signs and Meaning in the Cinema.* Bloomington: Indiana University Press, 1969.

Chapter Five

Uses of Extracts in Genre Study

A variety of approaches to the study of genre exists for the teacher. In my own film courses we have studied the following genres: the Western, comedy, science fiction, musical, and gangster film. In the unit on the Western, for example, we have viewed and studied closely: *Stagecoach, My Darling Clementine, Shane, Broken Arrow, Will Penny, High Noon, Lonely Are the Brave, Ride the High Country, The Rounders,* and *The Great Northfield Minnesota Raid.* In the unit on the musical comedy, however, we looked at only one film, *Singin' in the Rain,* as a microcosm of both the musical and comedy traditions in film. We have viewed *Public Enemy* as one example of the urban gangster film, and *Bonnie and Clyde* as an example of the rural gangster film—both of which framed a unit on the thematic concept of violence as it is treated in film and as it exists in society. In other units we identified and itemized the general elements of a specific genre, then applied them to one film—*Seconds* or *King Kong,* for example, in the science fiction category.

A broader filmic approach is to trace the elements of one genre across several cultures or nations. Consider, for example, the concept of the Western hero in such films as Howard Hawks' *Rio Bravo* (U.S.A., 1959), Akira Kurosawa's *Yojimbo* (Japan, 1961), and Sergio Leone's *Fistful of Dollars* (Italy, 1966). Other interesting comparisons might be Kurosawa's *Seven Samurai* (1954) with John Sturges' later version of the same theme, *The Magnificent*

Extracts in Film Study

Seven (1960); or Kurosawa's *The Stray Dog* with Don Siegel's *Coogan's Bluff*, both of which deal with the police genre.

Another approach, used in a 1972 workshop on "The Gangster Film" given by Professors Stuart Kaminsky, John Cawelti, and Gerald Temaner, compared the literary version of Ernest Hemingway's short story, "The Killers," with the two film versions—Robert Siodmak's *The Killers* (1946) and Don Siegel's *The Killers* (1964). This approach is rewarding because one can discuss, among many other options, how the two different media treat similar content and how the reader and viewer respond to these differences.

These approaches, or ways of using feature films, could easily be enhanced and expanded with extracts. Again, as in Chapter One, I would like to discuss the extracts selected for this project and make some suggestions as to their use in the study of film. These ideas are more descriptive than prescriptive, more suggestive than dogmatic, and are by no means exhaustive of the teaching possibilities. I repeat that these extracts were selected from those which were available, through special permission, from Films Incorporated. Not all of their films were available for this project. In fact, after we had selected and annotated several extracts, permission to take extracts from the features was not granted. I have already described the project as we conceived and fulfilled it. Even without the extracts, however, the suggestions that follow can be helpful in teaching a course on the genre film. As an initial program, no more than two features were selected for each genre; in several genres, however, many features could have been used since we viewed more than 200 films during the project. Thus, certain films in some of the genres are more representative than others.

No attempt was made on the selectors' part to establish an orthodoxy in teaching film. The selection of extracts, however, is not a neutral activity. It involves two kinds of judgments: (1) a critical judgment, both about the value of the film itself and about which sequence to select; and (2) an educational judgment about the relative value of particular kinds of curriculum or course organization. We realized that as the provision of materials—especially in a new field like film—can, to some extent, determine teaching practice, it is important that film selection be pluralistic and take account of any reasonably substantial critical and educational view. The selections are merely one other way of approaching the study of film; in addition, they are a breakthrough (in this country) in providing more filmic tools.

The extracts that follow are similar to those of the British Film Institute in that they are organic, unedited internally, and oriented to both form and content. They range over such major genres as the Western, comedy, science fiction, musical, and gangster films that Hollywood has produced so well from the 1920s to the 1960s. Because we were convinced of the importance of film study in the schools, we selected the extracts primarily for teachers of film; they also can be used to great advantage by teachers of English, social studies, psychology, communications, and humanities.

After a preliminary viewing of many films, the first two films listed in each of the following genres were finally selected for extracts. The titles in parentheses are those of other films which were seriously considered as being representative of a particular genre.

The Western:	*The Gunfighter*
	My Darling Clementine
	(Ride the High Country)
	(Wagonmaster)
	(Stagecoach; 1939 version)
	(Bad Day at Black Rock)
The Musical:	*Singin' in the Rain* (See Appendix V)
	The Gay Divorcee
	(Flying Down to Rio)
	(On the Town)
	(Funny Face)
Science Fiction:	*The Day the Earth Stood Still*
	The War of the Worlds
	(The Thing)
	(Forbidden Planet)
	(Planet of the Apes)
	(The Time Machine)
	(When Worlds Collide)
Comedy:	*The Cameraman* (See Appendix V)
	Monkey Business (Hawks)
	(A Night at the Opera)
	(I Was a Male War Bride)
	(Bringing Up Baby)
	(The Family Jewels)

(Knock on Wood)
(MGM Parade of Comedy)

Gangster-Detective: *Murder My Sweet*
The St. Valentine's Day Massacre

(The Asphalt Jungle)
(The French Connection)
(Shaft)
(Point Blank)
(Party Girl)

Horror: *King Kong*
Dr. Jekyll and Mr. Hyde (Mamoulian)

(The Thing)
(Mephisto Waltz)
(The Other)

An example of the British approach to the use of extracts in teaching film may be found in Appendix I, through the kind permission of the editor of *English in Education* and the author, Daniel Millar of the Department of Film and Television at Bede College in Durham, England.

Chapter Six

Genre: The Western

The two films from which extracts were selected in this genre are John Ford's *My Darling Clementine* (1946) and Henry King's *The Gunfighter* (1950). (The two back-up films were John Sturges' *Bad Day at Black Rock* and Sam Peckinpah's *Ride the High Country.*)

For each film in this and the following five chapters, a synopsis of both the feature and the extract is given, along with a listing of the cast and credits, and suggestions for classroom use.

MY DARLING CLEMENTINE (1946) 20th Century-Fox

DIRECTOR: John Ford
PRODUCER: Samuel G. Engel
SCRIPT: Samuel G. Engel, Winston Miller; from a story by Sam Hellman, who adapted Stuart N. Lake's book, *Wyatt Earp, Frontier Marshal*
PHOTOGRAPHY: Joe MacDonald
ART DIRECTORS: James Basevi, Lyle R. Wheeler
MUSIC: Alfred Newman
EDITOR: Dorothy Spencer
CAST: Henry Fonda—Wyatt Earp
        Victor Mature—Doc (John) Holliday
        Cathy Downs—Clementine Carter

The clash of cultures is represented in Wyatt Earp (Henry Fonda) from the West and in Clementine Carter (Cathy Downs) from the East in *My Darling Clementine*. (Twentieth Century-Fox 1946. Directed by John Ford. A-B, FI)

Linda Darnell—Chihuahua
Walter Brennan—Old Man Clanton
Tim Holt—Virgil Earp
Ward Bond—Morgan Earp
Don Garner—James Earp
John Ireland—Billy Clanton
Grant Withers—Ike Clanton
Ben Hall—Barber
Russell Simpson—John Simpson

Plot Synopsis

Wyatt Earp and his two brothers, Virgil and Morgan, become marshal and deputies of Tombstone, Arizona, to avenge the murder of their brother James and the rustling of their cattle herd. As marshal, Earp is gradually drawn into the life of the town and reaches a compromise with "Doc" Holliday, who dominates the town. The romantic interest in the film revolves around a dance-hall girl, Chihauhua, who is in love with Doc, and Doc's fiancée from the East, Clementine, who instead falls in love with Wyatt Earp. With Doc's help, Wyatt and Morgan outduel the Clantons, who were responsible for the murder of two brothers. All the Clantons and Doc are killed, and Earp leaves town after promising Clementine that he will return.

Extract: 14 minutes

The setting is Tombstone on a bright Sunday morning. Wyatt Earp receives a haircut, relaxes on a veranda, talks with his brothers, and is invited to a dance the town is holding to celebrate the building of the church. He reluctantly refuses; but when Clementine appears and asks him to go, he escorts her through the town to the dance. Intercut is a scene in a hotel room in which Doc decides to marry Chihuahua.

Discussion

This extract is a good example of some basic concerns of the Western genre, Ford's philosophy about the West, and the role of Wyatt Earp in the film as a whole. In regard to the first element, many Westerns have dealt with a concept of the West which Henry Nash Smith, in his significant book *The Virgin Land*, characterizes as both savage desert and pleasant Garden of Eden. This concept is typified by Tombstone and its surroundings. In this particular scene from the film, we see Wyatt Earp, the film's hero, gravitate from those characteristics of the untamed wilderness to those of civilized society. We see Earp impeccably attired in a dark suit, shaven, doused with honeysuckle perfume (which is incorrectly identified twice as being a fresh, natural scent), scanning himself in front of a mirror as his coat is brushed by the barber. Bells ring both to welcome people to church and to usher in a major civilizing influence. All these details accumulate to suggest a definite break from Earp's nomadic and wild past to a more civilized and stable present. Ford suggests, with subtlety, the influence of civilization on the frontier past.

Even though as an individual Earp is still bent on revenge for his brother's murder (a recurring motivating element in Westerns), he is now the upstanding sheriff who must perform the important role of maintaining law and order in the community. Ford's idea of the necessity of locating an ideal community amidst the stark wilderness of Monument Valley (a setting which the director used in at least eight other films: *Stagecoach, Fort Apache, She Wore a Yellow Ribbon, Wagonmaster, Rio Grande, The Searchers, Sergeant Rutledge,* and *Cheyenne Autumn*) is beautifully filmed in this extract, which is climaxed by shots of the exuberant, robust dancing of Earp and Clementine on a rough floor, juxtaposed with those of the vast, savage wilderness in the far background and of the wooden framework of the church tower in the near background. The skeleton form of the church is a regenerative spark for both the town and Earp. The harmonious vision of a primitive, epic wasteland and an emerging civilization is perfectly symbolized by the coupling of Earp of the West and Clementine of the East, a union of nature with culture.

Ford follows the Western genre pattern by using his female characters to typify the clash of cultures: on the one hand, he presents the virtuous, refined, pure, civilized Clementine, from Boston, who is always primly dressed in high-necked, buttoned blouses or jackets; on the other, he shows us the erotic, experienced, voluptuous, independent Chihuahua, from the saloon, who, in a low-cut blouse, flaunts her sexuality while trying to marry Doc. Doc has fled the East and all it represents and ventured to the West to escape. He uses the West, its gambling, its drinking, its whoring, as a haven from his failure in the East. Doc is ambivalent in that he expresses the limitations of civilization and, at the same time, reaffirms the basic elements of what the town represents. Both his alienation and his commitment to the town and Earp serve as a foil to Earp's developing awareness of his own role as avenger and upholder of the law. As Doc chooses Chihuahua in the hotel room and Earp chooses Clementine in the dance scene, Ford presents a microcosm of choices about accepting or forsaking ways of life: Doc chooses the natural, savage life with its accompanying regret and tragedy (he dies at the film's end); Earp reaches out for the cultured, civilized life.

A strong sense of community and tradition is poetically and lovingly created by Ford through a number of details: the family on the buckboard welcoming Earp, the stately Earp joining in the dance, the lively musicians, and the American flags in the foreground. The marriage-like walk by Earp and Clementine to the dance, as well as the dance itself, provides a confident assurance, an imaginative intensity, and an affectionate lyricism that epitomize the whole romantic, relaxed style of Ford's films and his nostalgic attitude toward America.

Fonda's acting lends a reserved nobility and quiet humanity to the legendary character of Earp, as evidenced in both the dance and the brief veranda scene in which Earp, on a chair, balances himself against a post. Earp, in talking at leisure with his brothers Morgan and Virgil about their home and Pa, also suggests another of Ford's basic themes: that of centering on the unity of the family both to establish stability in the community and to effect dynamic change of a savage environment. In fact, the critic John Baxter, in *The Cinema of John Ford*, states: "Regular and slowly-eaten meals, neat clothing, quiet conversation and easy movements make them (the Earps) the embodiment of conscious control and the law they represent." This familial theme is more clearly realized in its contrast to the Clanton family, headed by Old Man Clanton (Walter Brennan), whose members are characterized by self-interest, greed, and chaos in the community. The Earp character functions in a most important role for the Western as mythic romance in that he becomes the archetypal hero who dominates both his environment and other men, yet who retains his individualism and sense of community by partaking in the rhythms and rituals of life in Tombstone. As John Cawelti (in *The Six-Gun Mystique*) describes the hero, Earp stands between civilization and savagery.

The extract can be used in a variety of ways. Along with the feature, or by itself, it can serve as a close study of Ford's themes and visual style. With other films, like *The Iron Horse, Stagecoach, Wagonmaster*, or *The Man Who Shot Liberty Valance*, it can typify a phase in the development of the Western as a genre and the changes in a director's attitude toward his work. It can be used with a feature from another director, such as Sam Peckinpah's *Ride the High Country* or *The Wild Bunch;* Hawks' *Rio Bravo;* or

Jimmy Ringo (Gregory Peck) employs the fundamental icon of the Western—the gun—on Cliff Clark in *The Gunfighter*. (Twentieth Century-Fox 1950. Directed by Henry King. FI)

Boetticher's *The Tall T,* for comparison of an individual director's attitude toward the West.

The extract also could serve as an example of the variations in acting styles, the appeal to changing audiences, and the resilience and reverberation of the Wyatt Earp legend if it is compared with other films about Earp: Walter Huston in *Law and Order* (1931); Jon Hall in *Frontier Marshal* (1939); Richard Dix in *Tombstone* (1942); Joel McCrea in *Wichita* (1955); Burt Lancaster in *Gunfight at the OK Corral* (1957); James Stewart in *Cheyenne Autumn* (1964); James Garner in *Hour of the Gun* (1967); and Stacy Keach in *Doc* (1971).

In addition, the extract is well-suited to complement significant printed material used in a unit on the West: Henry Nash Smith's *The Virgin Land,* Richard W. Lewis' *The American Adam,* Jim Kitses' *Horizons West,* Robert Warshow's "The Movie Chronicle: The Westerner," and John Cawelti's *The Six-Gun Mystique.*

An interesting film to use in conjunction with either the excerpt or the full-length feature, *My Darling Clementine,* is a documentary produced by David Wolper, entitled *Shootout at OK Corral* (available from Wolper Productions, 8489 West Third Street, Los Angeles, California 90048. Rental fee—$75).

THE GUNFIGHTER (1950) 20th Century-Fox

DIRECTOR: Henry King
PRODUCER: Nunnally Johnson
SCRIPT: William Bowers, William Sellers; from a story by Sellers and André de Toth
PHOTOGRAPHY: Arthur Miller
MUSIC: Alfred Newman
EDITOR: Barbara McLean
CAST: Gregory Peck—Jimmy Ringo
      Peggy Walsh—Ringo's wife
      Millard Mitchell—Marshal Mark Strett
      Richard Jaeckel—Eddie
      Skip Homeier—Hunt Bromley
      Harry Shannon—First bartender
      Karl Malden—Second bartender (Mac)
      Jean Parker—Molly
      Hank Patterson—Jake
      Eddie Parkes—Barber
      D. G. Norman—Jimmie
      Alan Hale, Jr.—First Brother (Eddie's)

David Clarke—Second Brother
John Pickard—Third Brother
Helen Wescott—Peggy Walsh

Plot Synopsis

Jimmy Ringo is an aging gunfighter who is tired of his past and of being the target of every upstart gunman who hopes to gain an easy reputation as Ringo's killer. After Ringo kills a young punk in a fair fight in a saloon, he rides into another town, Cayenne, to try to persuade his wife and son to start a new life with him. Because three avenging brothers are on his trail, his arrival in town disrupts its normal activities: one man tries to ambush him, another challenges him to a duel, and the marshal, an old friend, orders him to leave town. His wife agrees to go with him, provided he serves out a year's test to prove his ability to fulfill his good intentions. As he prepares to leave the town, he is shot in the back by a young sharpshooter.

Extract I: 4 minutes, 30 seconds

Entering a saloon, weary gunfighter Jimmy Ringo tries to enjoy a leisurely drink but is confronted by a swaggering young upstart who taunts him into a gun battle. In a fair fight, Ringo kills Eddie (Richard Jaeckel) and leaves town.

Extract II: 10 minutes, 15 seconds

Hunt Bromley (Skip Homeier) comes to a barbershop, where he learns of Ringo's arrival at the saloon. Meanwhile, Eddie's three brothers are still making their way to town to avenge their brother's death. Bromley goes into the bar to provoke Ringo into a gunfight; Ringo bluffs him into thinking that he (Ringo) has a gun hidden under the table. Molly visits Ringo's wife and asks her about her attitude toward her husband. As they talk, Ringo's son escapes from his bedroom, where his mother had sent him to keep him out of harm's way.

Discussion

These two extracts can be used in a variety of ways. First, one can analyze the individual way in which King handles and refines certain elements of the Western genre: *e.g.*, the recurrent, typical ritual showdown. In the first extract, the swaggering arrogance and taunting childishness of "Fast Eddie" (Richard Jaeckel) are actions which foreshadow and almost beg for his death. While Eddie tries to egg Ringo into a fight by calling him "Mr. Frazzle-

The Western   47 bottom," Ringo exhibits reluctance and control of his gun. When he is forced to draw his gun, however, he does so with supreme skill, discipline, and detachment. The actual shooting is nicely photographed. We see Eddie draw and collapse; then the camera cuts to Ringo, his gun still smoking, to indicate his lightning-fast draw. Now that we, the viewers, know how skillful Ringo is, King ennobles Ringo in the second extract by having him outwit Hunt Bromley (Skip Homeier), who uses almost the same language to taunt Ringo into a duel. King plays on the audience's expectation of a blazing duel, but cleverly neutralizes that expectation by having Ringo bluff and humiliate Bromley rather than kill him. Contrary to the typical Western pattern of the gunfighter using his guns to do his talking, Ringo atypically uses language (the threat of a gun hidden under the table) to substitute for a violent confrontation. This action, of course, only exacerbates Bromley into shooting Ringo in the back at the film's end.

King's entire presentation, including the absence of the usual icons of the Western, is effectively manipulated. First, King refuses to use the typical exterior settings to create a mood of Western expansiveness and freedom. Instead, he pares down the vast topography of the West which usually evokes a sense of epic grandeur and the regeneration of its characters. In both of the extracts and throughout the full-length film, he presents either dark, cramped, stuffy interiors or bleak exteriors which restrict the characters rather than allowing them freedom to roam. Even in the two large saloons—which give the illusion of depth through the angle shots of the long bar—the dreary walls; dusty floors, mirrors, doors; and the physical texture of the faces of the minor characters, with their wrinkled clothes, all combine to envelop Ringo within a depressing atmosphere. King creates an environment of gloom in place of fecundity, limitation in place of openness; in effect, he reduces the terrain and simultaneously concentrates the action and intensifies the tragic situation of Ringo, as a Western hero, by internalizing the action of the individual. King accentuates this ominous mood and bleak reality through the film's subdued gray lighting, the ordinary chairs and tables in the Palace Bar, the dreary costume worn by Ringo, and even his black handlebar moustache which, on an actor like Gregory Peck, not only tends to age him but to add to his dignity. The glaring absence of music (except in the first extract) stresses King's attempt to demythologize the Western; viewers might contrast this absence of music with Ford's psychological use of the musical theme from *My Darling Clementine* as Earp, who is unconsciously

In a Western with a contemporary setting and theme Robert Ryan (right) confronts investigator Spencer Tracy in *Bad Day at Black Rock*. (MGM 1955. Directed by Robert Sturges. FI)

in love with Clementine, walks into the hotel while whistling that tune.

King uses some typical genre elements, such as the former bad man who is now reformed into the upright marshal (Mark Strett), the sympathetic saloon girl (Molly), and the peace-loving schoolteacher, all of whom act as foils to Jimmy Ringo. Molly's husband was killed, but Mark Strett made it—now maybe Ringo can, too.

King varies the genre use of the main character, however—the hero who resolves the basic external conflicts in a strange town. Instead, in the character of Jimmy Ringo, he presents a complex hero who has internalized the conflict between savagery and civilization. In King's film, the action centers not between good and evil, but between two sets of values—those of civilization and those of personal heroism in the old, wild West. It is this conflict whch makes Ringo a tragic figure. The character fulfills Northrop Frye's description of tragedy as a merging "of a fearful sense of rightness (the hero must fall) and a pitying sense of wrongness (it is too bad that he falls)." [1] King de-romanticizes the hero while celebrating the anti-heroic elements of the character's style. Ironically, Ringo's style is of no consequence in a time and place in which young killers care less for style than for a reputation.

Played with stoic restraint by Gregory Peck, Ringo is a disillusioned, anachronistic man who is beginning to sense the fact that he is out of step with his time. He must face an inevitable retreat as a gunfighter, or go through a resurrection of sorts by reuniting himself with his family and town. His past—never as romantic and heroic as he once dreamed it would be—is doomed, but he is faintly hopeful for the future. He is a gunman: alone, resigned, regretful; he is defeated not so much by the young gunman who is about to inherit his mistakes, but by the onslaught of time (the ticking of the clock and the close-ups of the clock in the bar are strong icons in the film). He represents a way of life that is becoming antiquated; the era of Western wilderness and lawlessness is over.

Yet in this first adult, psychological Western, Ringo—as the alienated loner—bears all this heavy awareness in a manner which ennobles him. His presence, throughout the extracts and the feature film, asserts itself, especially as the viewer watches Ringo's eyes, his stolid facial expressions, and the deliberate way in which he moves. Ringo is a man of violence who is now ashamed of his violent methods. His experiences parallel the slow-moving inevita-

[1] Northrop Frye, *Anatomy of Criticism* (Princeton, New Jersey: Princeton University Press, 1971), p. 214.

bility of a classical tragedy, in which he enacts the role of a doomed hero. Robert Warshow, in "The Movie Chronicle: The Westerner," aptly describes him: "What 'redeems' him is that he no longer believes in this drama and nevertheless will continue to play his role perfectly: the pattern is all." [2] Essentially, Ringo becomes an archetypal hero: the sacrificial scapegoat who atones for his past and reluctantly accepts his fate as a result of the conflict between the present civilization and his heroic past. And we sympathize with this tragic defeat of a man who still retains his dignity in ignominious death.

Bibliography

Amelio, Ralph. "The Western." *Film in the Classroom: Why Use It? How to Use It.* Dayton: Pflaum, 1971.

Anderson, J. L. "Japanese Swordfighters and American Gunfighters." *Cinema Journal,* XII (Spring, 1973).

Anderson, Lindsay. "John Ford." *Cinema* (American) (Spring, 1971).

————. "The Method of John Ford." *The Emergence of Film Art.* Ed. Lewis Jacob. New York: Hopkinson and Blake, 1969, pp. 23–245.

Armes, Roy. "The Western as a Film Genre," *Film and Reality: An Historical Survey.* pp. 141–149. Baltimore: Penguin, 1974.

Baxter, John. *The Cinema of John Ford.* New York: A. S. Barnes, 1971.

Bazin, André. *What Is Cinema?* Tr. by Hugh Gray. Vol. II. Berkeley: University of California Press, 1971.

Bogdanovich, Peter. *John Ford.* Berkeley: University of California Press, 1968.

Breihan, Carl W. *Great Gunfighters of the West.* San Antonio, Texas: Naylor, 1970.

Cawelti, John. *The Six-Gun Mystique.* Bowling Green, Ohio: Bowling Green University Press, 1970.

————. "The Jewish Cowboy, the Black Avenger, and the Return of the Vanishing American." *University of Chicago Magazine,* LXV (January/February, 1973).

Everson, William K. *The Pictorial History of the Western Film.* New York: Citadel, 1969.

Eyles, Allen. *The Western.* New York: A. S. Barnes, 1967.

Fenin, George. *The Western from Silents to the Seventies.* New York: Grossman, 1973.

[2] Robert Warshow, "The Movie Chronicle: The Westerner," *Film: An Anthology,* ed. Daniel Talbot (Berkeley: University of California Press, 1959), p. 99.

Ford, Dan. "The West of John Ford and How It Was Made." Action, VI (September/October, 1971), pp. 35–39.

Ford, John. Special articles in the following periodicals: *Film Comment* (Fall, 1971); *Films in Review* (January, 1969); *Focus on Film* (Spring, 1971); *Velvet Light Trap*, No. 2 (August, 1971).

Frantz, Joe B., and Julian E. Choate, Jr. *The American Cowboy: The Myth and the Reality.* Norman: University of Oklahoma Press, 1968.

French, Philip. *Westerns: Aspects of a Movie Genre.* London: Secker and Warburg, 1973.

French, Warren. "West as Myth: Status Report and Call for Action." *Western American Literature*, I (Spring, 1966), pp. 55–58.

Frost, Frank. "The Western: A Genre in Transition," *Films '69/'70*, National Catholic Office for Motion Pictures, pp. 45–48, 1971.

Hawgood, John A. *America's Western Frontiers.* New York: Alfred Knopf, 1967.

Hine, Robert V. *The American West: An Interpretive History.* Boston: Little, Brown & Co., 1972.

Homans, Peter. "Puritanism Revisited: An Analysis of the Contemporary Screen Image Western." *Studies in Public Communication*, No. 3 (Summer, 1961), pp. 73–84. Reprinted in *The Popular Arts in America: A Reader.* Ed. William M. Hammel. New York: Harcourt, Brace, Jovanovich, 1972.

Kaminsky, Stuart M. *American Film Genres.* Dayton: Pflaum, 1974.

_____. *Myth to Screen: A Genre Anthology.* Dayton: Pflaum, 1975.

_____. "The Samurai Film and the Western." *Journal of Popular Film*, I (Fall, 1972), pp. 312–324.

Kitses, Jim. *Horizons West.* Bloomington: Indiana University Press, 1970.

Lewis, R. W. B. *The American Adam.* Chicago: University of Chicago Press, 1955.

Lovell, Alan. "The Western." *Screen Education* (September/October, 1967, pp. 92–103.

Lyons, Peter. "The Wild, Wild West." *American Heritage* (August, 1960).

Manchel, Frank. "Archetypal American." *Media and Methods* (April, 1968).

_____. *Cameras West.* Englewood Cliffs, New Jersey: Prentice-Hall, 1971.

Maynard, Richard A. "John Ford and the American Image." *Scholastic Teacher* (January, 1974), pp. 28–30.

The Western

In a funeral scene typical in the Westerns, Van Heflin (center) prays over the coffin of a farmer shot in a conflict with cattlemen in *Shane*. (Paramount 1953. Directed by George Stevens. FI)

McArthur, Colin. "The Roots of the Western." *Cinema* (October, 1969), pp. 11–13.

McMurtry, Larry. "Cowboys, Movies, and Myths." *Man and the Movies*. Ed. W. R. Robinson. Baton Rouge: Louisiana State University, 1967.

Miller, Don. "New Words on Old Westerns." *Focus on Film* (Autumn, 1972).

Mostacci, John. "The American West." *Issues in American History: A Filmic Approach*. Dayton: Pflaum, 1975.

Nachbar, Jack. "A Checklist of Published Materials on Western Movies." *Journal of Popular Film*, II (Fall, 1973), pp. 411–428.

_____. "Seventy Years on the Trail: A Selected Chronology of the Western Movie." *Journal of Popular Film*, Vol. II (Winter, 1973), pp. 75–83.

Nachbar, Jack, ed. *Focus on the Western*. Englewood Cliffs, New Jersey: Prentice-Hall, 1974.

Parkinson, M., and C. Jeavons. *A Pictorial History of Westerns*. New York: Hamlyn, 1972.

Pechter, William S. "Anti-Western." *Twenty-Four Times a Second*. New York: Harper & Row, 1971, pp. 91–96.

Pratt, John. "In Defense of the Western." *Films and Filming*, I (November, 1954), p. 8.

Richards, Jeffrey. *Visions of Yesterday*. Henley, England: Routledge and Kegan, 1974. (On Ford)

Rieupeyrout, J. L. "The Western: A Historical Genre." *Quarterly of Film, Radio & T.V.* VII (1952).

Rosa, Joseph G. *The Gunfighter: Man or Myth?* Norman: University of Oklahoma Press, 1970.

Ross, T. J. "Fantasy and Form in the Western: From Hart to Peckinpah." *December*, XII (Fall, 1970), pp. 158–169.

Sadoul, Georges. *Dictionary of Films*. Berkeley: University of California Press, 1972.

Sarris, Andrew. *Interviews with Film Directors*. New York: Bobbs-Merrill, 1967.

_____. "The World of Howard Hawks." *Focus on Howard Hawks*. Ed. Joseph McBride. Englewood Cliffs, New Jersey: Prentice-Hall, 1972, pp. 55–58.

Scheide, F. "Mythicized Gunfighters of the Old West." *Velvet Light Trap*, No. 8 (1973), pp. 29–33.

Smith, Henry Nash. *The Virgin Land*. Cambridge, Massachusetts: Harvard University Press, 1970.

Steckmesser, Kent. *The Western Hero in History and Legend*. Norman: University of Oklahoma Press, 1965.

Thomas, Bob, ed. *Directors in Action.* New York: Bobbs-Merrill, 1973.

Tuska, Jon. *100 Finest Westerns.* Garden City, New York: Doubleday, 1975 (forthcoming).

Valdes, Joan, and J. Crow. "The Western Hero." *The Media Works.* Dayton: Pflaum, 1973.

Velvet Light Trap. "The Western" (entire issue devoted to the Western), No. 12, Spring, 1974.

Warshow, Robert. "The Movie Chronicle: The Westerner." *Film: An Anthology.* Ed. Daniel Talbot. Berkeley: University of California Press, 1959. (Also in *The Immediate Experience.* New York: Atheneum, 1970.)

Wecter, Dixon. *The Hero in America: A Chronicle of Hero-Worship.* Ann Arbor: University of Michigan Press, 1963.

Whitehall, Richard. "The Heroes Are Tired." *Film Quarterly,* XX (Winter, 1966–67), pp. 12–24.

Willett, Ralph. "The American Western: Myth and Anti-Myth." *Journal of Popular Culture,* IV (Fall, 1970), pp. 455–463.

Wood, Robin. *Howard Hawks.* Garden City, New York: Doubleday, 1968.

————. "Shall We Gather at the River? The Late Films of John Ford." *Film Comment,* VII (Fall, 1971), pp. 8–17.

Chapter Seven

Genre: Science Fiction

The two features extracted for the science fiction genre are *The Day the Earth Stood Still* (1951) and *The War of the Worlds* (1953).

THE DAY THE EARTH STOOD STILL (1951) 20th Century-Fox

DIRECTOR: Robert Wise
PRODUCER: Julian Blaustein
SCRIPT: Edmund H. North; based on the short story, "Farewell to the Master," by Harry Bates
PHOTOGRAPHY: Leo Tover
MUSIC: Bernard Herrmann
DESIGNERS: Lyle Wheeler, Addison Hehr
CAST: Michael Rennie—Klaatu
      Patricia Neal—Widow
      Hugh Marlowe—Fiancé of widow
      Sam Jaffe—Famous physicist
      Billie Gray—Widow's son

Plot Synopsis
A mysterious and ominous-looking white spaceship approaches the Earth at 4,000 miles per hour. It lands at the nation's Capitol and from it emerges a superior man, Klaatu, and his

mindless robot, Gort. They come from a planet (whose civilization is hundreds of years ahead of ours) some 250 million miles away. Klaatu tries to warn Earth's citizens that they must use their atomic weapons and power only for peaceful means. He is received with hostility and suspicion by most people, but is befriended by a young widow, her son, and a scientist. Klaatu demonstrates his great power by shutting off all sources of power in the world; for 30 minutes, everything ceases to move. After he is killed and resurrected, Klaatu and Gort leave Earth with a warning: control your aggressiveness or die.

Extract: 10½ minutes

The extract consists of the first minutes (the introduction) of the film. It opens with a long shot of the world and then a montage of flash reports of a strange object speeding toward the Earth. The flying saucer lands, with a terrifying whine, on the grass between the Washington Monument and the White House. For two hours it remains motionless while army tanks and heavy guns stand guard around its gleaming silver sides, which apparently have no doors, hatches, or openings. Then, suddenly, the ship's dome slides open, a ramp juts out, and Klaatu—a being who is human in appearance—steps out, followed by Gort. Klaatu states: "We have come to visit you in peace and good will." He is shot by a nervous soldier and Gort retaliates by disintegrating soldiers and nearby objects.

THE WAR OF THE WORLDS (1953) Paramount

DIRECTOR: Byron Haskin
PRODUCER: George Pal
SCRIPT: Barré Lyndon; based on the novel of the same name by
    H. G. Wells
PHOTOGRAPHY: George Barnes
MUSIC: Leith Stevens
ART DIRECTORS: Hal Pereira, Albert Nozaki
SPECIAL EFFECTS: Gordon Jennings, Wallace Kelley, Paul Lerpae,
    Ivy Burts, Jan Donela, Irmin Roberts
NARRATOR: Sir Cedric Hardwicke
CAST: Gene Barry—Professor Clayton Forrester
    Ann Robinson—Sylvia Van Buren
    Les Tremayne—General Mann
    Lewis Martin—Pastor Matthew Collins
    Charles Gemora—Martian

Plot Synopsis

To the accompaniment of an ominous voice-over by Sir Cedric Hardwicke, a series of beautiful long shots of planets is projected. We learn that the Martians are seeking to live on another planet because their planet and others in our solar system are uninhabitable. They invade Earth. Townspeople first think a meteor has struck, then discover that the "shooting star" actually is a spaceship containing a Martian invader. The film's characters—a professor of astro-nuclear physics, a minister, his niece, some scientific colleagues from Pacific Tech, and all the military—even by using the A-bomb cannot find a way to stop the Martian invaders. After mass destruction occurs across the world, the people panic and a holocaust engulfs Los Angeles. Life on this planet appears doomed, until bacteria kill off the enemy.

Extract: 19 minutes

The extract consists of two major scenes from the film: the first details the futile efforts of the military to destroy three Martian spaceships, and an attempt by the minister to communicate with the Martians. The second scene deals with the scientist and his girl friend, who are establishing a love relationship at a farmhouse when spaceship crashes into the house and traps them. In an encounter with a Martian, the scientist hacks off one of the creature's TV lenses with an ax. Both characters are able to escape from the house before it is destroyed by the Martian.

Discussion on both extracts

The two films chosen to represent the science fiction genre were produced in the 1950s—*The Day the Earth Stood Still* in 1951, and *The War of the Worlds* in 1953—a decade when science fiction films mushroomed along with the nation's nuclear tests and research. The Fifties recorded the proliferation of such films as *Destination Moon* (1950), *When Worlds Collide* (1951), *The Thing* (1951), *Them!* (1953), *Godzilla* (1955), *Invasion of the Body Snatchers* (1956), and many others. In contrast to previous science fiction films like *Metropolis, The Lost World,* and *King Kong*— which dealt with future societies, prehistoric preserved environments, and jungle giants—the films of the 1950s not only embellished the usual conventions of the genre but added a few of their own inventions.

As usual, the films contained the typical elements of the genre, as established by H. G. Wells and Jules Verne: the positive and negative sides of scientific investigation; space journeys to new

Two significant icons, the spaceship and the space robot (Gort), dominate the frame in *The Day the Earth Stood Still.* (Twentieth Century-Fox 1951. Directed by Robert Wise. FI)

worlds and strange cultures; time travel to the past, the future, and the fourth dimension; and visits from representatives of alien cultures (usually a super-race), sometimes friendly, but more often hostile. A number of real-life inventions contributed to the vitality and energy of the genre during the 1950s, however; the inventions ranged over such areas as politics, psychology, and the humanities in addition to (of course) science. Essentially, the science fiction films of the Fifties reflected, in varying degrees of explicitness, the basic concerns and fears of mass society in America. One major elemental fear struck a universal chord—fear of the unknown and of the future. On a specific level, political paranoia ran rampant in the decade, with McCarthyites finding a Communist under every bed and expecting a Russian invasion any day. At the same time, a psychological fear that plagued many people was that of the "Bomb" and its disastrous, destructive potential.

Susan Sontag, in a masterful essay entitled "The Imagination of Disaster," [1] discusses two significant aspects of the science fiction film: the threat and execution of destruction on a mass scale. She details both the imagery and the aesthetics of destruction, which often center on scientific knowledge. In fact, man's attitude toward science and scientists at this period of history was ambivalent: he both admired the promise of scientific advancement and dreaded its potential catastrophic power. From the bombing of Hiroshima and Nagasaki he could see that the A-bomb had "saved" him from Axis domination; but since 1945 he had been afraid that other international powers (Russia and China) would have the very same power to obliterate him. Thus, from a humanistic point of view, man was greatly concerned with his very existence and survival.

The two extracts from *The Day the Earth Stood Still* (abbreviated as *DESS* from this point on) and *The War of the Worlds* embody the central genre conventions of science fiction films. In *DESS* the presentation of setting, characters, themes, icons, and mood are well-treated as genre elements. Washington, D.C., the very center of international power, is invaded by aliens from another planet. Hysteria and panic ensue, as visualized in the usual montage of newscasters' reports, military response, and suspenseful music. The human characters are minimized and, for the most part, are one-dimensional. Instead, the "super" characters, with their spaceship as a looming icon, dominate both the frame and

---

[1] Susan Sontag, "The Imagination of Disaster," *Against Interpretation* (New York: Dell, 1969).

Science Fiction

the film: the shiny 9-foot robot, Gort—with its stolid anthropoid features and a body as seamless as its flying saucer—combines with the bleak black and white photography to establish the film's grim, tense tone. The obvious superiority of the spaceship, Gort's power, and Klaatu's intelligence increase man's feeling of vulnerability—and fascinate him, as well. Man now realizes what Galileo made evident long ago: no longer is he at the center of the universe; and he fears this fact. Yet, at the same time, he is enthralled by the awesome, wonderful knowledge that a superior being is visiting *him*.

This ambivalence also is reflected in the film's treatment of its theme. Man is immediately hostile to these aliens, but, as we soon see, he should be friendly and welcome them, since Klaatu comes with a beneficial message: Live in peace or face destruction. Do not continue to test your nuclear weapons because they are endangering others in the galaxy. Yet, as both Carlos Clarens (in *An Illustrated History of the Horror Film*) and Professor Stuart Kaminsky (in a taped lecture) suggest, Klaatu—as a Christ-figure on an important mission—is scorned, shunned, and attacked. Man is his own enemy and he suffers tragic results: immediately, with Gort's violent response to the attack on Klaatu, and more long-range results in the cessation of communications with a superior people, and the possibility of ultimate and inevitable annihilation.

The War of the Worlds (abbreviated as *WW*) also makes brilliant use of the conventions of the science fiction genre. Again, the extraterrestrial forms of life are sophisticated and intelligent beyond our imagination, but in this case they are brutal and violent. Here, the fear of the unknown is fulfilled in the most frightening manner: the spaceships incinerate man, leaving only carbonized ashes in their wake. Instead of visiting Earth with a warning, the Martians have come to take over; they not only invade, but they deprive man of his existence with their exterminating death ray. The invasion of the quiet town of Santa Mira, California, is a microcosm of what is happening internationally in the film.

This extract has an appeal on both a mass and an individualized scale. On a mass level, the military with all its manpower and vast firepower (including the A-bomb which is used later in the film) tries vainly to stop the dogged onslaught of the Martian spaceships. This scene is most effective in its striking sounds and images of destruction—the eerie humming, the snake-like antennae attached to the manta ray-shaped machines hovering over the Earth, and the screeching blast of the Martian death ray—

which reach their climax in the jolting medium shot of a soldier who is disintegrated, before our eyes, in a dazzling maze of colors. Thus, the military is unable to save man.

On an individualized level, the religious element in the film, in the form of a minister, is also unable to help man. The minister foolishly attempts to communicate with the Martians by reading them the 23rd psalm. As the camera tracks him, his words, "I shall not fear . . ." are ironic; he is quickly obliterated into nothingness while the constant, eerie, pulsating sound of the Martian machine increases. The fear felt by the film's audience now has assumed gigantic proportions: this evil power is indestructible. Nothing can stop the invaders.

On an even more individualized level, the main characters—the scientist and his girl friend—are enmeshed in a web of science fiction and horror conventions. In a quiet moment of the film, Sylvia recalls her love for her uncle in a scene reminiscent of a budding love story. But they soon find themselves trapped in an isolated house when a Martian spaceship crashes into it. It is dark, strange sounds pervade, the composition of the frame is chaotic and cluttered with broken beams, the girl is frightened, and the scientist is tense. As the house is scanned by the probing three-eyed TV lens and searched by an actual Martian, the scientist—relying on the simplest of tools (an ax)—beats off the Martian in one-to-one combat and beheads its TV lens. One can barely glimpse the Martian; thus the suggestion of horror becomes more effective than the statement of it.

These three purposeful, deliberate, and seemingly rational responses to the threat presented by the Martian invaders are dynamic contrasts to the film's actual ending. For it is not military, scientific, religious, or individual human power which defeats them. The solution is accidental and inscrutable: nature, through a simple bacteria, renders the alien creatures helpless.

The two representative science fiction films, and their extracts, owe much of their creativity and powerful visualizations to the special effects men (Gordon Jennings and George Pal in *WW*), the cinematographers (Leo Tover in *DESS* and George Barnes in *WW*), and the sound director (Bernard Herrmann in *DESS*) who worked under the direction of Byron Haskin, in *WW*, and Robert Wise, in *DESS*. Both films have tightly-knit, rapid, action-packed narratives which make significant statements on such science fiction themes as the threat of superior knowledge and the precarious sense of individual existence. Both films fulfill the dual function of science fiction films: they allow the audience to indulge in escapist fantasies while they simultaneously neutralize horror, terror, and fear through a catharsis of those feelings. Both films end with an apocalyptic denouement: man's place on Earth is relative. In one film, he is saved from Armageddon by a mere whim of nature; in the other, he awaits his doom—unless he changes his war-like ways.

An interesting compilation film to use along with these extracts and a full-length genre feature is *Science Fiction Anthology* (40 min.; CFS), with clips from old and new science fiction films: *It Came from Outer Space*, *The Lost World* (silent), *Tarantula*, and *The Incredible Shrinking Man*.

Bibliography

Amelio, Ralph J. *Hal in the Classroom: Science Fiction Films.* Dayton: Pflaum, 1974.

Baxter, John. *Science Fiction in the Cinema.* New York: A. S. Barnes, 1970.

Bradbury, Ray. "If I Were a Teacher." *Learning: The Magazine for Creative Teaching*, Vol. 1, No. 7 (May, 1973), pp. 14–17.

Calkins, Elizabeth, and Barry McGhan. *Teaching Tomorrow: A Handbook of Science Fiction for Teachers.* Dayton: Pflaum, 1972.

Chappell, Fred. "The Science-Fiction Film Image," *The Film Journal*, Vol. 2. No. 3 (Issue 6, 1974), pp. 8–13.

Clarens, Carlos. *An Illustrated History of the Horror Film.* New York: Capricorn Books, 1968.

Clareson, Thomas D., ed. *SF: The Other Side of Realism.* Bowling Green, Ohio: Bowling Green University Press, 1971.

Durgnat, Raymond. "The Wedding of Poetry and Pulp—Can They Live Happily Ever After and Have Many Beautiful Children?" *Films and Feeling.* Cambridge, Massachusetts: M.I.T. Press, 1967.

The Film Journal, "The Science Fiction Film Image" (entire issue devoted to science fiction film) Issue 6, Vol. 2, Number 3, 1974.

Gifford, Denis. *Science Fiction Film.* London: Studio Vista/Dutton, 1971.

Hodgens, Richard. "A Brief, Tragical History of the Science Fiction Film." *SF: The Other Side of Realism.* Ed. Thomas D. Clareson. Bowling Green, Ohio: Bowling Green University Press, 1971, pp. 248–262.

Hollister, Bernard C., and Deane C. Thompson. *Grokking the Future: Science Fiction in the Classroom.* Dayton: Pflaum, 1973.

Houston, Penelope. "Glimpses of the Moon." *Sight and Sound*,

XXII (April/June, 1953), pp. 185–188.

Jensen, Paul. "H. G. Wells on the Screen." *Films in Review*, XVIII, (November, 1967), pp. 521–527.

Johnson, Dennis S. "The Five Faces of George Pal." *Cinefantastique* (Fall, 1971), pp. 5–27.

Johnson, William, ed. *Focus on the Science Fiction Film*. Englewood Cliffs, New Jersey: Prentice-Hall, 1972.

Jonas, Gerald. "Onward and Upward with the Arts: SF." *The New Yorker* (July 29, 1972), pp. 33–51.

Kaminsky, Stuart M. *American Film Genres*. Dayton: Pflaum, 1974.

Koch, Howard. *The Panic Broadcast*. New York: Avon Books, 1970.

Landrum, Larry. "A Checklist of Materials about Science Fiction Films of the 1950's: A Bibliography." *Journal of Popular Film*, Vol. I No. 1 (Winter, 1972), pp. 61–63.

Lee, Walt, ed. *Reference Guide to Fantastic Films: Science Fiction, Fantasy, & Horror*. Three volumes. Los Angeles: Chelsea-Lee Books, 1972.

Livingston, Dennis. "Schooling Up for a Future with the Futurists." *Media and Methods* (March, 1973), pp. 26–29, 70–71.

Miller, David C. and Peter Schwartz. "16mm Measures the Future: Futures Films Update" and "Science Fiction Feature Films." *EMC One-74*, (pp. 14–19). *(Berkeley, California: University of California Extension Media Center, 1974.)*

Millies, Suzanne. *Science Fiction Primer for Teachers*. Dayton: Pflaum, 1974.

Murphy, Brian. "Monster Movies: They Came from Beneath the Fifties." *Journal of Popular Film*, Vol. I No. 1 (Winter, 1972), pp. 31–44.

Sobchack, Vivian. "The Alien Landscapes of the Planet Earth," *The Film Journal*, Vol. 2, No. 3 (Issue 6, 1974), pp. 18–21.

Sontag, Susan. "The Imagination of Disaster." *Against Interpretation*. New York: Dell, 1961, pp. 212–228.

Steinbrunner, Chris, and Burt Goldblatt. *Cinema of the Fantastic*. New York: Saturday Review Press, 1972.

Waldron, Edward E. "Science Fiction, Movies and Freshman English: All for One and One for All." *Arizona English Bulletin* ("Films and the English Class" issue), Vol. 13, No. 2 (February, 1971), pp. 18–23. (Available from Ken Donelson, English Department, Arizona State University, Tempe, Arizona 85281. $1.50.)

Willis, Don. *A Checklist of Horror and Science Fiction Films*. Metuchen, New Jersey: Scarecrow Press, 1972.

A conventional situation in science fiction films occurs here with the military confronting the robot Gort in *The Day the Earth Stood Still*. (Twentieth Century-Fox 1951. Directed by Robert Wise. FI)

Chapter Eight

Genre: Horror

The two extracts we selected to represent the horror genre are from *Dr. Jekyll and Mr. Hyde* (1932) and *King Kong* (1933).

DR. JEKYLL AND MR. HYDE (1932) Paramount

DIRECTOR: Rouben Mamoulian
PRODUCER: Rouben Mamoulian/Adolph Zukor
SCRIPT: Samuel Hoffenstein, Percy Heath; based on the novel of
    the same name by Robert Louis Stevenson
PHOTOGRAPHY: Karl Struss
ART DIRECTOR: Hans Dreier
CAST: Fredric March—Dr. Henry Jekyll/Mr. Hyde
      Miriam Hopkins—Ivy Pearson
      Rose Hobart—Muriel Carew
      Holmes Herbert—Dr. Lanyon
      Edgar Norton—Poole, the servant
      Halliwell Hobbes—Brigadier General Carew
      Arnold Lucy—Utterson

Plot Synopsis
    In a fine introduction, using a mobile and subjective camera, the film shows Dr. Jekyll as he delivers a controversial lecture dealing with the separation of the nature of man. Later Dr. Jekyll,

who is engaged to Muriel, the daughter of the upper-class Brigadier General Carew, aids an attractive young woman named Ivy, who has been beaten up. As he experiments with his controversial idea, he does, in fact, separate himself into a second nature—that of Mr. Hyde, a brutal, animalistic man. Hyde terrorizes Ivy and eventually kills her. After several more transformations, Hyde attempts to kill Muriel and does manage to kill her father. He is then hunted down by Dr. Lanyon and the police, and is shot to death in his laboratory. As he dies, he is transformed again into his first nature—that of Dr. Jekyll.

Extract: 15 minutes

Dr. Jekyll is on his way to his engagement party at the home of his fiancée, Muriel. In the park, a nightingale's lyrical chirping leads him to sit beneath a tree. Suddenly, his second transformation begins. As Hyde, he goes to Ivy's house, abuses her for trusting Dr. Jekyll, and then kills her. He escapes to Dr. Lanyon's house, where he is transformed again while Lanyon watches, aghast. As Jekyll, he confesses all to Lanyon and promises to destroy the potion.

Discussion

Mamoulian's *Dr. Jekyll and Mr. Hyde* is one of the finest examples of the horror genre. In this particular extract, he epitomizes several recurring elements of the genre: the brutal actions of a human monster; the brilliant use of light and shadow to provide atmosphere and mood; the symbolic use of decor and objects; the magical potion; the psychological appeal of unleashed power, fury, and unconscious lust; and the confrontation of good and evil, externalized by Dr. Jekyll, which is felt within all people.

The extract and the film achieve their power through Mamoulian's handling of the theme of the duality and polarity in human nature, as expressed both in the schizophrenic character Jekyll/Hyde and in the contrasting of opposites in the film. In the extract we see the happy, handsome, confident Dr. Jekyll, who is about to be married, become transformed into the hideous, savage, bestial Mr. Hyde, who is about to kill; at the end of the scene, the desperate Mr. Hyde transforms himself back into the abject, humiliated Dr. Jekyll. The transformations parallel the extremes of the character's feelings of love. Natural, normal love for Muriel elevates Jekyll, at the beginning of the extract, into a man of supreme happiness and lively energy. As he walks through the park, he feels close to nature and to the chirping nightingale. The abrupt cessation of the bird's chirping (in the original story, a cat attacks it) seems to trigger Jekyll's personality change. In addition, however, the long repression of his love—which was forced upon him, through an extended engagement, by Muriel's father—has perverted Jekyll's love and propelled his Hyde-nature into sadism and murder of Ivy (and, eventually, of Muriel's father). For Hyde, sex and violence are equated and interchangeable. His repressed feelings of love also energize Jekyll into his pathetic confession to Dr. Lanyon at the end of the extract.

These transformations—changes in personality, or nature—are remarkable both thematically and technically. As in many films of this type, Jekyll—the proud, vibrant, and idealistic scientist—has unleashed a force so powerful that, in the words of Dr. Lanyon, it "has conquered" him. Earlier in the film, Jekyll says that the thing one can't do always tempts him. Typically, he no longer can control what he has created. The theme of complete loss of control of one's creation has been a significant one in both literature and film, most notably in Mary Shelley's novel and James Whale's film, *Frankenstein*. The Jekyll/Hyde transformations allow Mamoulian to stress and isolate the tragic results of one man's warring schizophrenic personalities. Mamoulian himself has said that the conflict here is not simply between good and evil, or moral and immoral, but rather between the spiritual and the animal—two elements which all men possess. Man cannot escape from his animal nature, but he should attempt to control it. Hyde's sadistic killing of Ivy is a result of Jekyll's inability to dominate his wild, primeval urges. Therefore, as Hyde revels in rape, mayhem, and murder, Jekyll himself rapidly retreats into atavism. His deterioration is symbolically suggested in the extract when, as he is about to drink the potion, the small candle in the right foreground flickers: the light of human knowledge wavers against the pervading darkness of Hyde in the background.

This scene also stresses the genre convention of the brilliant but deranged scientist who invents a miraculous potion. Just as potions have been used in various ways throughout literature (by Virgil's Dido, Shakespeare's Juliet and King Claudius, and Wagner's Isolde, for example), so has Mamoulian's film made use of man's desire for a magical mixture which can separate the aspects of his personality. As is usual in the horror film genre, Mamoulian uses such icons as the smoking concoctions in laboratory beakers and bottles.

Technically, both of the character transformations in this extract are brilliant: they are shown in horrifying close-up, achieved through an ingenious blend of lighting, filters, and make-up (a unique process which, even today, Mamoulian has not revealed). Stuart Kaminsky, in his discussion of the film,[1] states that Mamoulian also makes inventive use of the split screen technique to suggest the idea of a split personality in society. A wipe moves across the screen diagonally, stopping at midscreen. In one half of the picture, we see Hyde walking away from the camera—a dark exterior background shot; in the other half, we see the party—a bright exterior shot. The next split screen shows Ivy and Muriel, the two women who represent opposite poles of Jekyll's desire: Ivy, blonde-haired, lower-class, and erotic, appears in the top frame; Muriel, dark-haired, upper-class, and reserved, in the lower frame.

Mamoulian's superb use of chiaroscuro (the contrast between areas of light and shade) highlights the duality of the characterization of Jekyll and the theme of the film. As a principle of good composition, the center of the film frame is bright enough to capture the viewer's attention, while the periphery is darker. Ivy's death scene, for example, centers on the white statue of Canova's Winged Psyche, tenderly holding the relaxed Eros, while the outer frame is grey. The shot becomes a marvelous counterpoint to the off-screen action of the vicious Neanderthal Hyde, strangling the struggling Ivy.

KING KONG (1933) RKO

DIRECTOR: Ernest B. Schoedsack, Merian C. Cooper
PRODUCER: Ernest B. Schoedsack, Merian C. Cooper
EXECUTIVE PRODUCER: David O. Selznick
SCRIPT: James Creelman, Ruth Rose; from a story by Merian C. Cooper and Edgar Wallace
PHOTOGRAPHY: Edward Lindon, Verne Walker, J. O. Taylor
SPECIAL EFFECTS: Willis O'Brien
MUSIC: Max Steiner
EDITOR: Ted Cheesman
DESIGN: Carroll Clark, Al Herman
CAST: Fay Wray—Ann Darrow
    Robert Armstrong—Carl Denham
    Bruce Cabot—Jack Driscoll
    Frank Reicher—Captain Englehorn
    Sam Hardy—Weston

[1] In a cassette available from Films, Inc.

Plot Synopsis

Carl Denham, a film producer, selects Ann Darrow for a role in his new picture, which he refuses to discuss with anyone. Jack Driscoll is first mate on a ship that carries them to mysterious Skull Island near Sumatra. There they find a native village dominated by a huge wall, outside which the villagers periodically offer a maiden as a sacrifice to appease the anger of a monster-god. The natives kidnap Ann from the ship and offer her to the monster. The rescue party is confronted by King Kong, a 50-foot ape, who escapes to his jungle kingdom. A series of conflicts in the jungle follows: the party kills a Stegosaurus; their raft is overturned by a Brontosaurus; Kong dislodges all the men except Driscoll from a log lying across a chasm; Kong defeats a Tyrannosaurus rex, a huge snake, and a pterodactyl. During the last fight, Driscoll rescues Ann and they escape to the village. Kong follows, barges through the gate, and tears up the village—only to be felled by the gas bombs thrown by Denham. Returning to New York, Denham displays Kong in a theater. Kong escapes in search of Ann, terrorizes the city, and finally is shot down by airplane bullets.

Extract: 18 minutes

Kong, the "eighth wonder of the world," as shown on a marquee, is being displayed in a New York theater. Denham introduces Kong to the public and photographers, then announces Ann's engagement to Driscoll. Kong then breaks loose and goes on a rampage of the city, seeking Ann. He smashes walls and "el" trains, and scales the tallest building in New York—carrying Ann. After he puts Ann down on a ledge, airplanes attack and eventually cause him to fall to his death.

Discussion

The extract, as well as the film, can be used in several ways.

● First, it is a marvelous example of the special effects wizardry of Willis O'Brien. Using more than 20 models of different sizes, with rubberized skin coated with animal hairs for Kong and scale-sized constructions of Kong's hand and face, O'Brien animated Kong by shooting a single film frame of every fraction of the creature's movement. Thus, two or three minutes of actual footage used in the film required days of shooting. Students who are involved in animating film can look carefully at this film as one of the finest examples of animation.

● Second, the extract is the logical conclusion of an exciting narrative/melodrama/fairy tale of beauty and the beast. The story it-

The "Beauty and the Beast" motif is evident in Mr. Hyde's (Fredric March) terrorizing the lovely Ivy (Miriam Hopkins) in *Dr. Jekyll and Mr. Hyde.* (Paramount 1932. Directed by Rouben Mamoulian)

self is admirably presented. The first third of the film is a perfect example of the use of formula elements to build up the tension of the exposition. For example, as Denham the entrepreneur discovers the penniless beauty, Ann, and as the love relationship between Ann and Jack Driscoll develops, the emphasis is put on the film's dialogue; the scenes are static, and no dynamic action is evident. The film develops slowly, with scenes foreshadowing the future: on the ship, Ann, in a provocative white gown, poses with a monkey (a smaller version of Kong) while Denham coaches her to act frightened. The eerie atmosphere is heightened by a misty fog and muted tom-toms.

Once Ann is kidnaped by the natives, the action accelerates while the dialogue decreases. As the great chase begins, action-packed scenes of fights among prehistoric beasts, Kong, and the rescue party follow. Visually, these are exciting, and the suspense is increased by Max Steiner's percussive music. The turning point occurs when Kong is felled by gas bombs and carted off to New York.

The chase motif is sustained as Kong escapes from Denham and wreaks havoc on the city. The climax comes when Kong has scaled the Empire State Building, only to be shot down by the planes. The denouement is a quiet epitaph delivered by Denham.

● Third, the extract can be interpreted as a social commentary. The film was released in 1933, the peak of the Great Depression, when 12 million people were jobless. Rightly or wrongly, those who inhabited and controlled the upper echelons of Wall Street, New York City, and the East were held responsible for this mass, debilitating chaos. Kong's willful destruction of the city is a visual attempt to act as a catharsis for the feeling of frustration and helplessness on the part of the vast majority who suffered during these times. Yet Kong, as a symbol of these oppressed workers and as a jungle bumpkin in the city, is taken advantage of by Denham, the city huckster who brings Kong as "a show to gratify your (audience) curiosity"; by the sophisticated, bejewelled audience which pays to see Kong exploited; by the "gentlemen of the press" who cruelly frighten Kong with their flashbulb cameras; and by the airplanes, the dynamic symbol of man's knowledge and ability to overcome gravity.

When *King Kong* is viewed as an example of social commentary, its racial overtones and stereotypes are both implicit and explicit. The island's native chief offers Denham six black girls in exchange for the one fair-skinned, blonde girl to appease (seduce) the black super beast, Kong. The natives are afraid of the white

In one of the best horror-monster films, King Kong (as himself) dominates both the frame and the entire film even though here he is temporarily restrained. (RKO 1933. Directed by Merian C. Cooper and Ernest B. Schoedsack. FI)

man's power—guns and bombs. Kong is supreme in his own jungle; but he is tricked by whites, shanghaied in chains on a boat to civilization, exploited and emasculated by whites (as is seen in the famous long shot of Kong on a steel cross in the Broadway theater). The film's unconscious racism, however, may be merely a reflection of the typical handling of black-white relationships at that time.

King Kong also is laden with erotic and sexual imagery, if one wishes to seek it out. Kong himself can be interpreted as a representation of the repressed libido and baser animalistic instincts of man, long contained behind walls in the jungle but now unleashed, in full fury, upon the city. Kong, with his strange semi-human features, gestures, and motivations, becomes a mighty symbol of man's atavistic impulses and Dionysian dynamism. Phallic icons abound, both in the jungle sequences (a fallen log used as a bridge; a huge tree on which Kong places Ann; the twin poles to which Ann is chained; the gigantic beam that locks the gate) and the city sequences (especially the Empire State Building). All of the imagery assumes the filmic guise of a dream—or a nightmare— in which such Freudian elements as long falls (by Ann and Jack into water, and Kong onto the street), exhilarating and frustrating chases through tangled jungles and dark city streets, and the whole erotic and suspenseful tension of Kong's pursuit and possession of Ann play a strikingly significant role in the film's appeal. Once the 50-foot Kong has captured Ann, his ritual bride, what can he possibly do with her?

● Finally, the film and its extract are a classic representation of the horror film in that they contain several genre conventions and inventions. Giantism has always had a peculiar fascination for audiences and, certainly, the towering Kong fulfills that convention. Kong also is an example of the creature who is discovered, corrupted, and then is unable to be controlled by its discoverer or society. Typically, he runs amok and must be destroyed.

One of the most basic conventions of the horror film is the "beauty and the beast" motif, which is immediately introduced in the credits: ". . . the beast looked upon the face of beauty." This convention is accentuated as the beast (Kong) pursues, captures, loses, and recaptures beauty (Ann Darrow), while the hero (Jack Driscoll) is reduced to a minor role. The conflict is essentially an external one of good against evil. Visually, this conflict is shown with Ann Darrow representing beauty, goodness, and purity in blonde hair (actually a wig), white diaphanous gowns, and very light makeup while, of course, Kong represents ugliness, evil, and lust in basic black. The beast is defeated by the "hero," civilization, and its modern power only after Kong futilely attempts to fight in the same way as he did in the jungle: he smashes an elevated train (snake), scales the Empire State Building (Skull Mountain), and knocks down a plane (pterodactyl).

One of the unique qualities of this film, however, is the director's "invention" of making the Kong character sympathetic to the audience, for surely—in his own way—he loves Ann. Rescuing her from the "attack" of the photographer's snapping flashbulbs and Jack Driscoll's caress, Kong never releases her until, in a beautifully tragic gesture, he gently places her on the ledge of the Empire State Building and bids her farewell. This convention is neatly summarized when Denham, looking at the dead Kong, says, "It was beauty killed the beast."

King Kong's popularity continues today, not only because of its "campiness." It is one of the best of the horror genre films, possibly because it fulfills man's desire to be frightened, to dream, and—by projection—to participate in the monster's wanton rampaging of civilization and attempted ravishing of the bride.

An interesting introduction to the horror genre might be a nostalgia reel, *Famous Movie Monsters* (45 min.; CFS; $150), which contains excerpts from the horror features *Frankenstein, Dracula, The Mummy, The Wolfman,* and *The Creature from the Black Lagoon.*

Bibliography

Ackerman, Forrest J. *The Frankenscience Monster.* New York: Ace, 1969.

―――. *Famous Monsters of Filmland.* New York: Warren Publishing Co., 1958.

Amelio, Ralph J. *Hal in the Classroom: Science Fiction Films.* Dayton: Pflaum, 1974.

Atkins, Thomas. "Dr. Jekyll & Mr. Hyde, an Interview with Rouben Mamoulian." *The Film Journal,* Vol. 2 (November 2, 1973), pp. 36–44.

Aylesworth, Thomas G. *Monsters from the Movies.* Philadelphia: J. B. Lippincott Co., 1972.

Bergman, Andrew. *We're in the Money: Depression America and Its Films.* New York: New York University Press, 1971.

Butler, Ivan. *The Horror Film.* Cranbury, New Jersey: A. S. Barnes, 1967.

―――. *Horror in the Cinema.* New York: Paperback Library, 1971.

Casty, Alan. *Development of the Film.* New York: Harcourt, Brace, Jovanovich, 1973.

Clarens, Carlos. *An Illustrated History of the Horror Film.* New York: Capricorn Books, 1967.

Crowther, Bosley. *The Great Films: Fifty Golden Years of Motion Pictures.* New York: G. P. Putnam's Sons, 1967.

Dillard, R. H. W. "Even a Man Who Is Pure at Heart." *Man and the Movies.* Ed. W. R. Robinson. Baton Rouge: Louisiana State University Press, 1967.

Douglas, Drake. *Horror.* Toronto: Collier Books, 1969.

Evans, Walter. "Monster Movies: A Sexual Theory." *Journal of Popular Film,* II (Fall, 1973), pp. 353–365.

Eyles, Allen, Robert Anderson, and Nicholas Fry. *The House of Horror: The Story of Hammer Films.* London, England: Lorrimer, 1974.

Gifford, Denis. *Movie Monsters.* New York: Dutton, 1969.

_____. *A Pictorial History of Horror Movies.* New York: Hamlyn, 1973.

Gow, Gordon. *Suspense in the Cinema.* New York: A. S. Barnes, 1968.

Harryhausen, Ray. *Film Fantasy Scrapbook.* New York: A. S. Barnes, 1972.

Higham, Charles, and Joel Greenberg. *The Celluloid Muse: Hollywood Directors Speak.* New York: Signet, 1969. (Mamoulian)

Huss, Roy, and T. J. Ross, eds. *Focus on the Horror Film.* Englewood Cliffs, New Jersey: Prentice-Hall, 1972. (paperback)

Jacobs, Lewis. *The Rise of American Cinema: A Critical History.* New York: Teachers College Press, 1969.

Kauffmann, Stanley, with Bruce Henstell. *American Film Criticism: From the Beginnings to 'Citizen Kane.'* New York: Liveright, 1972.

Lennig, Arthur, ed. *Classics of the Film.* Madison: Wisconsin Film Society Press, 1965.

"Mamoulian on His *Dr. Jekyll and Mr. Hyde.*" Tr. by Bill Thomas. *Cinefantastique* (Summer, 1971), pp. 36–38.

Manchel, Frank. *Terrors of the Screen.* Englewood Cliffs, New Jersey: Prentice-Hall, 1970.

Matthews, J. H. *Surrealism and Film.* Ann Arbor: University of Michigan Press, 1971.

Milne, Tom. *Rouben Mamoulian.* Bloomington: Indiana University Press, 1969.

Murphy, Brian. "Monster Movies: They Came from Beneath the Fifties," *Journal of Popular Film,* Vol. I, No. 1 (Winter, 1972).

Robert Mulligan ironically uses the innocence of children (Martin and Chris Udvar-noky) in the horror thriller *The Other*. (Twentieth Century-Fox 1972. Directed by Robert Mulligan. From the Thomas Tryon novel.)

O'Brien, Willis. "Creator of the Impossible." (A full career study of the animator of *King Kong* and *The Lost World.) Focus on Film*, No. 16 (Fall, 1973).

Pirie, David. *A Heritage of Horror: The English Gothic Cinema 1946–1972*. England: Gordon Fraser, 1974.

Sarris, Andrew, ed. *Hollywood Voices*. New York: Bobbs-Merrill, 1971.

_____. *Interviews with Film Directors*. New York: Bobbs-Merrill, 1967.

Steinbrunner, Chris, and Burt Goldblatt. *Cinema of the Fantastic*. New York: Saturday Review Press, 1972.

Willis, Donald C. *Horror and Science Fiction Films: A Checklist*. Metuchen, New Jersey: Scarecrow Press, 1972.

Wolf, Leonard. *Monsters*. San Francisco: Straight Arrow Books, 1974.

Fear and violence are staples of the horror genre as portrayed here with a dog at-
tacking the beautiful Paula (Jacqueline Bisset) in *The Mephisto Waltz*. (Twentieth
Century-Fox 1971. Directed by Paul Wendkos. From the novel by Fred M. Stewart.)

Chapter Nine

Genre: Film Noir (Detective)
and
Gangster Film

The two features extracted for the film noir-gangster genres are *Murder My Sweet* (1945) and *The St. Valentine's Day Massacre* (1967).

MURDER MY SWEET (1945) RKO

DIRECTOR: Edward Dmytryk
PRODUCER: Adrian Scott
SCRIPT: John Paxton; based on Raymond Chandler's novel *Farewell, My Lovely*
PHOTOGRAPHY: Harry J. Wild
MUSIC: Roy Webb
ART DIRECTION: Albert S. D'Agostino, Carroll Clark
EDITOR: Joseph Noriega
CAST: Dick Powell—Philip Marlowe
     Claire Trevor—Helen (Velma)
     Anne Shirley—Ann Grayle
     Otto Kruger—Jules Amthor
     Mike Mazurki—Moose Malloy
     Ralf Harolde—Dr. Sonderberg
     Miles Mander—Mr. Grayle

Philip Marlowe (Dick Powell) as a loner private eye at the mercy of Moose (Mike Mazurki) and his henchman in *Murder My Sweet.* (RKO 1944. Directed by Edward Dmytryk. FI)

Plot Synopsis

Philip Marlowe, his eyes bandaged because of gunshot wounds, recounts in flashback for the police his most recent job. First he is asked by ex-con Moose Malloy to find his girl, Velma; then he is asked by a wealthy old man and his young blonde wife to recover a valuable jade necklace. While attempting to accomplish both of the above, he encounters numerous obstacles, including Malloy himself, the suave but mysterious Amthor, and the "femme fatale," Helen. With the help of Ann Grayle, daughter of Mr. Grayle, Marlowe discovers that Helen and Velma are the same girl—and that she stops at nothing, including murder, to gain her end. She is shot by her husband, who is then killed by Malloy. Marlowe, still blindfolded, rides away with Ann in a taxi.

Extract: 18 minutes

Malloy meets Marlowe in a nightclub and convinces him to visit with Amthor. While there, Marlowe engages Amthor in some confusing but witty dialogue about the missing jade necklace and Amthor's nefarious dealings. When Marlowe refuses to tell Amthor all he knows about the necklace, Amthor has Malloy strangle him; eventually, he has Marlowe drugged. Marlowe experiences hallucinatory nightmares but, through a supreme effort of his will, overcomes the drug, his attendant captor, and the "doctor" of the house, and escapes.

Discussion

Murder My Sweet belongs to a controversial genre that the French have labeled "film noir" (the black or dark film), a development of the detective, gangster, sociological, and documentary films of the 1930s. Briefly, film noir is really not a genre, but a film style which stresses certain motifs and tone, is delineated by a definite visual style, and exists in a definite period of film history. Crime, criminals, and corruption are the central motifs of these films; the tone is cynical, sinister, and depressing; the settings are those of contemporary (1940–1950) urban life with its gloomy, shabby areas—dingy rooms, dark, wet streets, and neon-lighted diners. The film noir style is seen in such Hollywood films of the 1940s and early 1950s as *The Maltese Falcon, Laura, The Naked City, Call Northside 777, They Live by Night, Brute Force, Double Indemnity, The Big Heat, Kiss of Death, Kiss Me Deadly, Touch of Evil, White Heat, The Big Sleep,* and *Sunset Boulevard.* Paul Schrader, in his influential article "Notes on Film Noir,"[1] lists four con-

---

[1] Paul Schrader, "Notes on Film Noir," *Film Comment* (Spring, 1972).

Typical confrontation in a gangster film occurs between hero (Robert Taylor) and armed villain (John Ireland) with mob boss (Lee J. Cobb) and chorus girl (Cyd Charisse) standing by, in *Party Girl*. (MGM 1958. Directed by Nicholas Ray. FI)

ditions in Hollywood during the 1940s which brought about film noir: war and post-war disillusionment, post-war realism, the influence of German expatriate directors, and the tradition of hard-boiled novelists and screenwriters.

To a large degree, the hard-boiled tradition accounts for the narrative power of *Murder My Sweet;* the author of the novel, Raymond Chandler, was one of the writers who developed this tradition, along with Dashiell Hammett (creator of Sam Spade), Ernest Hemingway (author of "The Killers" and *To Have and Have Not*), James M. Cain (author of *Double Indemnity*), and Horace McCoy (author of *They Shoot Horses, Don't They?* and *Kiss Tomorrow Goodbye*). More recently, this tradition has been continued by Ross Macdonald (in his Lew Archer series) and perverted by Mickey Spillane (author of the Mike Hammer series).

These novelists contributed heavily to the development of the conventions for the "noir" detective film: the tough, cynical hero who possesses an individualistic code of romanticism, loyalty, and decency; the beautiful but cunning "femmes fatales"; the frightening and brutal villains who appear as minor characters; the complex, convoluted plots which stress a quest of some sort; the staccato, ironic, and realistic dialogue; the nostalgic flashbacks (Schrader suggests that the overriding theme of film noir is a passion for the past and present, and a fear of the future); a fatalistic, hopeless mood; the confining, depressing, and authentic settings; and the sardonic, stoic philosophy—a foreshadowing of existentialism—which is epitomized in Chandler's statement: "It is not a very fragrant world, but it is the world you live in. . . ."

The icons and settings of film noir are strongly influenced by German expressionism. The urban jungle of streets, alleys, offices, and barrooms is lit for night, and almost always is somber, stark, and menacing; the composition of the film frame is a mass of confusing, restrictive, oblique, and sharp angular lines which express the insecurity, tension, and fear of the characters, their environment, and situations. The atmospheric cinematography establishes a baroque visual style which affects the spectator's attitude toward the characters and enhances the expression of the director's themes of violence, pessimism, corruption, and disillusionment.

Murder My Sweet includes a variety of "noir" detective conventions. In addition to the usual icons of the seedy, urban environment of Marlowe's office and several bars, and the luxurious upper-class settings of Mr. Grayle and the amoral Amthor, the most sinister icon is a physical one: Moose Malloy. His towering hulk and foreboding power, shot from a low angle with low-key lighting, suggest the oppressive, savage reality that Marlowe must confront.

The whole extract is part of a long flashback which Marlowe is recounting to the police in an attempt to explain a complicated case involving four deaths, a missing jade necklace, and several bumps on his head. The settings in the extract are all filmed at night; they switch quickly from a crowded nightclub to a confining secret elevator, and from the fancy high-rise apartment of the psychic consultant, Jules Amthor, to a dingy room in Dr. Sonderberg's mausoleum-like house. From the spectator's—and Marlowe's—point of view, the progression of events is fragmented, bewildering, and nightmarish, especially in the scene of Marlowe's being drugged, which begins with his wry voice-over: "a black pool opened up at my feet. . . ." The drugging scene is significantly expressionistic in touching on a number of aspects which are characteristic of the entire film: the fuzzy grey spider web superimposed on the fleeting images Marlowe sees, for example, is reflective of the confusion of the whole circumstance of events; and the frustrating, helpless falling of Marlowe, who is never really in control of the situation, suggests his alienation and futility in trying to solve the murders. The sleazy "hospital" room itself is suggestive of the claustrophobic, oppressive composition of both the film itself and film noir. Marlowe recovers from the debilitating drug and escapes from the dark room only when he is able to overcome the effects of the drug by the sheer force of his own will power. This action by him becomes a microcosm for the solution to the whole film, in that he alone untangles the murder mysteries. At the same time, he becomes a hero for the audience because he uncovers and confronts the fear, despair, loss of identity, and paranoia which are present in a post-war, tawdry, amoral world. Los Angeles, as a setting for the "American dream," has atrophied into the "American nightmare."

Typical of the detective of the 1940s, Marlowe is alone in a corrupt asphalt jungle and is at the mercy of clever and brutal villains. Even though he is betrayed by women, tricked by his client, beaten up by a wealthy, mysterious sharpie, and drugged by a "doctor" (whom Marlowe calls "Dr. Jekyll"), he doggedly survives and eventually solves the case and wins the beautiful girl—all without the aid of the police. The luring of Marlowe by Moose Malloy to Amthor's apartment is done explicitly (by the fearful hugeness of Moose) and implicitly (in the appeal to Marlowe's sense of loyalty and duty to complete the job Moose has paid him for). Cruelty and force become much more explicit when Moose and the chauffeur pull guns on Marlowe in the elevator, when Moose chokes Marlowe, and when Amthor hits Marlowe across the face with a gun. Yet Marlowe, as a cynical "noir" hero, survives in this moral wasteland—possibly because he is self-sufficient. He is a loner, both because the romantic hero is doomed to solitude and because he may be better than the environment he inhabits. The high society of Amthor, Grayle, and Dr. Sonderberg, is morally bankrupt, and the police are inept. Through the mire of lies, double-crosses, beatings, and murders, Marlowe adheres to his own code, retains his integrity, and becomes a hero archetype on a symbolic quest to restore some balance and meaning to the moral order. Chandler himself describes his detective: "Down these means streets a man must go who is not himself mean, who is neither tarnished nor afraid. He is the hero; he is everything."

A Selected Bibliography of Readings and Films on the Private Eye as Genre

● Prototype: Humphrey Bogart as Sam Spade in *The Maltese Falcon* (1941), directed by John Huston, based on Dashiell Hammett's novel.

● Two other versions of this novel exist: *The Maltese Falcon/ Dangerous Female* (1931), directed by Roy Del Ruth, with Ricardo Cortez as Spade; and *Satan Met a Lady* (1936), directed by William Dieterle, with Warren Williams as Spade.

● Other films based on Raymond Chandler's novels:
The Lady in the Lake (1946), directed by Robert Montgomery, who also played the part of the Marlowe character;
The Big Sleep (1946), directed by Howard Hawks, with Marlowe played by Humphrey Bogart;
The Blue Dahlia (1946), directed by George Marshall and featuring Alan Ladd;
The Brasher Doubloon (1947), directed by John Brown and featuring George Montgomery;
Marlowe (The Little Sister) (1968), directed by Paul Bogart and featuring James Garner; and
The Long Goodbye (1973), directed by Robert Altman and featuring Elliot Gould.

● Other popular versions of the private eye genre can be found in the following films:

Lee Marvin as the ominous avenger is out to destroy the mob in the 1967 gangster film *Point Blank!* (MGM 1967. Directed by John Boorman. FI)

William Powell in *The Thin Man* (1934) and other films in this
series;

Ralph Meeker in *Kiss Me Deadly* (1955);
Paul Newman in *Harper* (1966);
Frank Sinatra in *Tony Rome* (1967);
George Peppard in *P. J.* (1969);
Richard Roundtree in *Shaft* (1971);
Rod Taylor in *Darker Than Amber* (1971);
Albert Finney in *Gumshoe* (1973);
Craig Stevens as television's *Peter Gunn* (1959);
Robert Forster in *Banyon* (1972), on television; and
William Conrad in *Cannon* (1971), also on TV.

THE ST. VALENTINE'S DAY MASSACRE (1967) 20th Century-
Fox

DIRECTOR: Roger Corman
PRODUCER: Roger Corman
SCRIPT: Horace Browne
CINEMATOGRAPHER: Milton Krasner
MUSIC: Lionel Newman
EDITOR: William B. Murphy
ART DIRECTION: Jack Martin Smith and Philip Jefferies
CAST: Jason Robards—Al Capone
      Ralph Meeker—Bugs Moran
      George Segal—Pete Gusenberg
      Clint Richie—Jack McGurn
      Joseph Campanella—Wienshank
      Richard Balalyan—Scalisi
      David Canary—Frank Gusenberg
      Harold J. Stone—Frank Nitti
      Paul Richards—Charles Fischetti
      John Agar—Dion O'Banion

Plot Synopsis
The film opens with the sounds of the massacre on February
14, 1929, which took place in a garage on Chicago's North Side.
The rest of the film is told in flashbacks by a voice-over narrator
who describes the background, the characters, and the events
leading up to the climactic death scene which is graphically pic-
tured at the end of the film. The film details the growing war over
control of bootlegging and gambling operations in Chicago be-

tween Al Capone's mob and the North Side mob of Bugs Moran (previously run by Hymie Weiss and Dion O'Banion). One brutal scene escalates into another until Bugs Moran orders the execution of Patsy Lalordo in order to make Joey Aiello the leader of the Sicilian mob, and to ensure that Capone will be left out. Capone retaliates by having Jack McGurn organize the massacre of Bugs, only to have seven men—but not Bugs Moran—murdered. The film's final irony is that not one member of Capone's mob was arrested for that crime.

Extract: 12 minutes

The extract begins with the entrance of Al Capone to his headquarters and continues with a typical "business" meeting during which Capone becomes infuriated because Bugs Moran is gradually taking over the North Side bootleg operation. Capone recalls, in a flashback, the time when Hymie Weiss attacked his Cicero hotel headquarters; he now cites this attack as a warning that Bugs is out to kill him. The scene ends as Jack McGurn is given the responsibility of killing Bugs Moran.

Discussion

Historically, the film recounts the violence and antiestablishmentarianism of the 1920s and simultaneously reflects those same themes of the 1960s (the Kennedy assassinations, college disturbances, the Vietnam War, racial-urban disorders, and antiwar demonstrations). From the point of view of genre and myth, the film and the extract deal with the rituals and conventions of the gangster film; in particular, the elevation of the gangster to epic stature.

In the first few minutes of the extract, Corman introduces the hero to his audience by using the iconography of the genre: the urban setting, big black car, tough bodyguards, flashy clothing, and, specifically, Al Capone with his expensive cigar, wide-brimmed fedora, and scarred face. The icons echo those of the gangster films of the 1930s: *Underworld* (1927) with George Bancroft; *Little Caesar* (1930) with Edward G. Robinson; *Public Enemy* (1931) with James Cagney; *Scarface* (1932) with Paul Muni and George Raft; *Bullets or Ballots* (1936) with Humphrey Bogart. Corman uses these icons, as well as the stylized color cinematography and the meticulous sets, to set the stage for the grand entrance of the emperor of the underworld and to function as trappings of brute power and tokens of easily identifiable success to the audience. Along with the visuals, the voice-over "March of

Time" narrator marshals biographical facts about Al Capone which add documentary authenticity to the myth of Capone as Public Enemy/Hero Number One.

Capone was part of American social history both then and now, and Corman develops this idea by treating him as both a legendary hero and a sadistic parody of the Horatio Alger-American success myth (Capone rose to the top of his profession in six short years). As a historical reconstruction film of the 1960s, along with Arthur Penn's *Bonnie and Clyde* (1967) and *Bloody Mama* (1969), the director merges a semi-documentary and an epic approach to his subject matter. Capone is god-like, supreme, and wrathful. He physically dominates each film frame and usually is photographed from a low angle. Even though he is surrounded by fawning, protective underlings, he is alone and fearful of chaos and loss of power. As a pseudo-businessman, he abides by the rules of American business: he holds executive board meetings, is concerned over cut-throat competition, and desires quick, profitable expansion of his product. His product, of course, is crime—which he sees not as a perversion but as part and parcel of the American system of success.

The board meeting in a plush hotel, with neatly arranged chairs, long, shiny table, and reserved atmosphere, is a grotesque parody of the typical corporate business meeting: before Capone arrives at least two brief conversations by Charles (The Fixer) Fischetti, Jake Guzik, and Frank (The Enforcer) Nitti deal with police and political corruption. Jake (Greasy Thumb) Guzik is first on the meeting's agenda, with a progress report laden with statistics, money figures, and grosses on sales of bootleg beer on the South Side. Capone himself, as the dynamic leader, dominates the meeting by flying into a hysterical rage over Moran's "unethical" methods (Moran's hoods shot Tony Lombardo, who was not even carrying a gun). And "Machine Gun" Jack McGurn, cool and reserved in front of his elders, exhibits the characteristics of an ambitious young executive in his thorough dossier on Bugs Moran. Capone makes it clear that he wants his monopoly over Chicago not only to endure, but to flourish.

The grim irony of the scene exists in the twisted ethics of these free entrepreneurs, since the decisions they make center on human life or death. No matter how brutal the violence, it is presented coldly and factually in the film. The flashback during the board meeting (showing Peter Gusenberg calmly shooting up Capone's Hawthorne Hotel headquarters in Cicero in October of 1926, in broad daylight) accentuates the callous violence of the pe-

The detective genre continues to flourish with the addition of films like *Shaft*, played by Richard Roundtree (with gun). (MGM 1971. Directed by Gordon Parks. From the novel by Ernest Tidyman.)

Two versions of the "big caper" film, a sub-genre of the gangster film, use the same dividing-the-jewelry scene. The original version is *The Asphalt Jungle* (right) and the newer version is *Cool Breeze* (left). (*The Asphalt Jungle* MGM 1950. Directed by John Huston. FI./*Cool Breeze* Gene Corman Production 1972. Directed by Barry Pollack.)

riod and the virtual non-existence of, and contempt for, law and order. The conventional use of the funereal procession of black cars, the chattering machine gun, the screams, the shattering glass, the white fedora with its dark hatband, and the white handkerchief in George Segal's jacket pocket provides the necessary icons for the typical urban shoot-out. This scene escalates into the final bloodbath of seven murders at the end of the film. Capone, at the end of the board meeting, shows his satanic black humor when he replies to Jack McGurn's comment on the deaths of so many of Moran's men: "I'll send flowers."

In his bold attempt to control an amoral empire faced with anarchy, Capone becomes an ironic example of a strong-willed man trying to combat the disintegration of culture and business and to replenish the bankruptcy of democracy for the people of the Twenties and the Sixties with direct and brutal leadership.

Bibliography

Alloway, Lawrence. *Violent America.* New York: Museum of Modern Art, 1971.

Baxter, John. *The Gangster Film.* New York: A. S. Barnes, 1970.

_____. *Hollywood in the Thirties.* New York: A. S. Barnes, 1968.

Bergman, Andrew. *James Cagney.* New York: Pyramid Communications, 1973.

Brackett, Leigh. "From *The Big Sleep* to *The Long Goodbye* and More or Less How We Got There." *Take One,* Vol. 4, No. 1, 1974, pp. 26–28.

Cameron, Ian. *The Heavies.* New York: Praeger, 1969.

Cawelti, John, ed. *Focus on Bonnie and Clyde.* Englewood Cliffs, New Jersey: Prentice-Hall, 1973.

Chandler, Raymond. "The Simple Art of Murder." *The Art of the Mystery Story.* Ed. Howard Haycroft. New York: Grosset and Dunlap, 1946.

Davis, B. *The Thriller.* New York: Dutton, 1973.

Deming, Barbara. *Running Away from Myself.* New York: Grossman, 1969.

Durgnat, Raymond. "The Family Tree of the Film Noir." *Cinema* (British), No. 6–7 (August, 1970).

Everson, William K. "The Gangster Film." *Film Review.* Ed. F. Maurice Speed. London: W. H. Allen, 1969, pp. 69–70.

Everson, William K. *The Detective in Film.* New York: Citadel Press, 1972.

Flynn, Tom. "Three Faces of Film Noir." *Velvet Light Trap* (issue on "The Forties in Hollywood"), Vol. 5 (Summer, 1972).

"The Forties in Hollywood." *Velvet Light Trap*, Vol. 5 (Summer, 1972).

French, Philip. "Incitement Against Violence." *Sight and Sound* (Winter, 1967/1968).

Gabree, John. *Gangsters: From Little Caesar to the Godfather*. New York: Pyramid, 1973.

Gregory, Charles. "Knight Without Meaning" (on the films featuring the Philip Marlowe character). *Sight and Sound* (Summer, 1973), pp. 155–159.

Grella, George. "Murder and the Mean Streets: The Hard-Boiled Detective Novel." *Contempora I* (March, 1970).

Higgins, George V. "The Private Eye as Illegal Hero." *Esquire* (December, 1972), pp. 348–351.

Kaminsky, Stuart M. *American Film Genres*. Dayton: Pflaum, 1974.

Karpf, Stephen. *The Gangster Film 1930–1940*. New York: Arno Press, 1973.

Koszarski, Richard. "The Films of Roger Corman." *Film Comment*, Vol. 7, No. 3 (Fall, 1971), pp. 43–48.

McArthur, Colin. *Underworld U.S.A.* New York: Viking Press, 1972.

Nye, Russell. "Murderers and Detectives." *The Unembarrassed Muse: The Popular Arts in America*. New York: Dial Press, 1970.

Place, J. A., and L. S. Peterson. "Some Visual Motifs of Film Noir." *Film Comment*, Vol. 10, (January/February, 1974), pp. 30–35.

Sacks, Arthur. "Analysis of Gangster Movies of the Early Thirties." *Velvet Light Trap*, No. 1 (1971).

Schrader, Paul. "Notes on Film Noir." *Film Comment* (Spring, 1972).

Sennet, Ted. *Warner Brothers Presents*. New Rochelle, New York: Arlington House, 1973.

Solomon, Stanley. *The Film Idea*. New York: Harcourt, Brace, Jovanovich, 1972.

"The Tough Guys of Film Noir." Six articles, *Film Comment*, Vol. X, No. 6 (Nov.–Dec., 1974), pp. 6–30.

Warshow, Robert. "The Gangster as a Tragic Hero." *The Immediate Experience*. New York: Atheneum, 1970.

Whitehall, Richard. "Crime, Inc.: A Three-Part Dossier on the American Gangster Film." *Films and Filming* (January/March, 1964).

Chapter Ten

Genre: The Musical

The two features we selected to extract are *The Gay Divorcee* (1934) and *Singin' in the Rain* (1952). (The film *Funny Face* is a substitute for *Singin' in the Rain*. See Appendix V, page 147, for details.)

THE GAY DIVORCEE (1934) RKO

DIRECTOR: Mark Sandrich
PRODUCER: Pandro S. Berman
SCRIPT: George Marion, Jr., Dorothy Yost, Edward Kaufman; from *Gay Divorcee* by Dwight Taylor
PHOTOGRAPHY: David Abel, with special effects by Vernon Walker
MUSICAL DIRECTION: Max Steiner, with dance ensembles by Dave Gould
SONG: "The Continental"; music by Con Conrad, lyrics by Herb Magidson
EDITOR: William Hamilton
ART DIRECTION: Van Nest Polglase and Carroll Clark
CAST: Fred Astaire—Guy Holden
      Ginger Rogers—Mimi Glossop
      Alice Brady—Hortense Ditherwell
      Edward Everett Horton—Egbert Fitzgerald
      Erik Rhodes—Rodolfo Tonetti

Eric Blore—Waiter
Lillian Miles—Hotel guest
Betty Grable—Hotel Guest

Plot Synopsis

Guy Holden (Fred Astaire), a professional dancer, meets Mimi Glossop (Ginger Rogers). Without even getting to know her name, he immediately falls in love with her. She is in the midst of getting a divorce, but needs a corespondent to fulfill the state's legal requirements. Her aunt (Alice Brady) knows a lawyer (Edward Everett Horton) who, incidentally, is a good friend of Guy's and who arranges to supply, as Mimi's corespondent, Rodolfo Tonetti (Erik Rhodes). Through a case of mistaken identity, Mimi believes Guy to be the hired corespondent. Eventually, all is worked out so that Guy and Mimi can get together.

Extract: 18 minutes

Tonetti is guarding both Guy and Mimi until the next day so that legally he can be judged as Mimi's corespondent. But Guy and Mimi, while watching a new dance of love, feel the urge to dance themselves. Guy sets up paper dolls on a record turntable, and places a light behind them to make it look as if he and Mimi are dancing in one room while Tonetti watches their "shadows" from another room. Then Guy and Mimi dance and watch others dance and sing "The Continental," with singing interludes by Erik Rhodes and Lillian Miles, and dance interludes by Eric Blore and about a hundred other dancers.

Discussion

As is usual in the musical genre film, the plot is of little significance—a fact which is glaringly evident in this film because the dance numbers and the talent of the characters stand out. In addition to the big production number at the climax of the film, "The Continental" (which won the first Academy Award in the best song category), Astaire and Rogers also sing and dance to Cole Porter's "Night and Day" earlier in the film.

This extract, which is one of the longest song and dance numbers in an Astaire film, is representative of the musical genre in several ways. First, the light comic motif is expressed through the minor characters, Rodolfo Tonetti (Erik Rhodes) and the dancing waiter (Eric Blore), both of whom perform the same kind of function in other Astaire musicals. Second, the production number itself is typical of most of the Thirties' musicals in that it takes place at the end of the film; features a variety of song and dance performances—by a group (of almost one hundred dancers and singers), a duet (Astaire and Rogers singing and dancing), and individual performers (singers Erik Rhodes and Lillian Miles); and is truly a visual spectacle enhanced by the striking interiors designed by art director Van Nest Polglase. The elaborate dance number is successfully achieved, for the most part, through the conscious directorial display of Mark Sandrich as he manipulates almost one hundred dancers in an imitation of Busby Berkeley's style: intricate geometric arrangements of large groups of dancers; rhythmic, mobile camera panning, tracking, and booming in and out of grandiose, elegant sets; montage-like cuts and dissolves; lavish black and white costumes and stunning costume changes on editing; sophisticated decor; and lyrical, flowing music with the orchestra largely unseen.

Third, and most significant in the musical genre, is the dancing of the main actors, Astaire and Rogers. Typical of the many musical plots in general, but more particularly in the Astaire-Rogers musical, is the kind of love relationship that exists and develops between the main characters. The plot centers on their contrasting personalities, as Astaire usually is in love/pursuit of her and she is antagonistic toward him. She is won over to him by means of his skillful dancing (as Astaire's films are dancers' musicals). In this extract, however, it is the song that triggers Astaire's expression of his love for Rogers; for, in it, one confides his secret love to his partner while they dance. Astaire makes an attempt in this scene to integrate song and dance with story and setting. It is Astaire-Rogers' dancing which becomes the visually exciting declaration of their love. As they dance in perfect synchronization, she in a white dress and he in a black tuxedo, they complement each other visually and belong together. Astaire's gestures with his hands, feet, and whole body and his ever-present tuxedo express the genius, elegance and charm of his personality—cool, debonair and supremely confident: characteristics consciously or unconsciously in demand when millions of men were unable to support their families during the hard years of the early 1930s.

Typically with Astaire films, the camera records but does not participate in the dance; it photographs the full figures of Astaire and Rogers in the frame at all times, and uses very few closeups. The song is cleverly integrated with the dance: as Lillian Miles sings of the countries where the "Continental" is done, Astaire and Rogers pantomime the song by dancing in Spanish flamenco, Hungarian gypsy, Viennese waltz, and American jazz styles.

The Musical

This film and its extract have an escapist appeal to an audience which was caught in the depths of a severe economic depression. The length and drive of the "Continental" number itself; the extravagant sets and costumes; the cooperation, precision, and unity of the dancers; and the sophistication, vitality, and sheer exuberance of Astaire and Rogers—all were attractive to the film audience of 1934.

SINGIN' IN THE RAIN (1952) MGM

DIRECTOR: Stanley Donen and Gene Kelly
PRODUCER: Arthur Freed
SCRIPT: Adolph Green and Betty Comden
PHOTOGRAPHY: Harold Rosson
PRODUCTION DESIGNERS: Cedric Gibbons and Randall Duell
MUSIC: Nacio Herb Brown and Roger Edens
LYRICS: Arthur Freed, Al Hoffman, Al Goodhart, Adolph Green,
        Betty Comden
CHOREOGRAPHY: Gene Kelly and Stanley Donen
EDITOR: Adrienne Fazan
COSTUMES: Walter Plunkett
CAST: Gene Kelly—Don Lockwood
      Debbie Reynolds—Kathy Selden
      Donald O'Connor—Cosmo Brown
      Jean Hagen—Lena Lemont
      Millard Mitchell—Simpson
      Cyd Charisse—A dancer
      Rita Moreno—Zelda Zanders
      Douglas Fowley—Roscoe Dexter
      Jimmy Thompson—Singer of "Beautiful Girl"

Plot Synopsis

Set in Hollywood in the 1920s, the film introduces two famous silent film stars who are teamed as a loving duo—dumb blonde Lena Lemont (Jean Hagen) and Don Lockwood (Gene Kelly). Although Lena believes that Don really loves her, he has, in fact, met a young, talented actress named Kathy Selden (Debbie Reynolds) and fallen in love with her. When the new sensation of the "talkies" is introduced to film, Don and Lena are teamed in their typical romance; but this time, as a talkie, it flops miserably—mostly because of Lena's voice. Cosmo Brown (Donald O'Connor) suggests that all can be saved if they dub in Kathy's voice to replace Lena's and re-make the film as a musical. All works well until

Lena discovers what is happening; she threatens to sue the studio, then attempts to force the producer, Simpson, to let her use Kathy as her singing voice without the public's knowledge. After the film premiere, while Lena is on stage, the audience requests her to sing an impromptu number for them. With Kathy behind the curtains singing for her, she mimes the words—as Don, Cosmo, and Simpson raise the curtain to reveal Kathy as the real singing star of the film.

Extracts: approximately 17 minutes

No. 1: consists of a sound montage introducing the talkies to the film world of the 1920s (1 minute, 57 seconds);

No. 2: consists of a behind-the-scenes rehearsal in which Don and Lena do the first takes for their talkie film. The rehearsal results in various recording difficulties, much to the frustration of the director, Roscoe Dexter (Douglas Fowley) (4 minutes, 16 seconds);

No. 3: consists of a love duet by Don Lockwood and Kathy Selden in a huge, deserted sound studio—"You Were Meant for Me" number (6 minutes, 30 seconds);

No. 4: consists of the title song, during which Don Lockwood, who is in love with Kathy, bids her goodnight and sings and dances in the rain until a bewildered policeman walks by (5 minutes).

Discussion

"I can't visualize it; I've got to see it on film." This line is said by the Hollywood producer, Simpson, to Don Lockwood (Gene Kelly) as Don tries to explain his concept of a musical number in the film *Singin' in the Rain*. The line also is apropos of any discussion of the four extracts from the film, especially the three which feature song and/or dance: they are difficult to discuss unless one has seen them, and even then their brilliance cannot be articulated too well.

The extracts can be used in a variety of ways. The extract (#2) showing Jean Hagen, Gene Kelly, Douglas Fowley, and Millard Mitchell rehearsing for their sound film is both historically accurate, in its depiction of the many difficulties which resulted from Hollywood's transition from silent to sound pictures, and wonderfully funny in its classic build-up to a comic climax. First, the director (who is in a sound recording booth) is unable to hear anything at all because neither actor is speaking toward the large

Fred Astaire, dancing as usual, is in "pursuit" of Ginger Rogers in this "Night and Day" duet from *The Gay Divorcee*. (RKO 1934. Directed by Mark Sandrich. FI)

microphone hidden in a nearby bush; then he is able to hear only every other word because Jean Hagen is moving her head back and forth. After the mike is sewn into the front of Jean's dress, the director hears only the thumping beat of her heart. Finally, the mike is sewn onto the shoulder of Jean's dress and is covered by a flower; the producer then barges onto the set, almost trips over the sound cord, yanks at it vigorously, and upsets Jean Hagen. A final cut to the director's frustrated face ends the scene. Ironically, what makes the whole scene funny is the uses of sound (especially Lena's voice) to build up the scene and then the director's climax of a sight gag, the standby of the silent film. This logical accumulation of details into a humorous conclusion is indicative of the careful construction given the entire film, and is another reason for the film's continued success and popularity.

The other three extracts are fine examples of musical conventions. The first is a montage-like spoof and tribute to the typical production numbers and routines in early musicals of the Busby Berkeley-Flo Ziegfeld style. The extract is quite accurate in that a great amount of experimentation came about with the introduction of sound to the musical. The "Beautiful Girl" number, with its full-dress fashion parade in lush MGM color, is nicely concluded with the Berkeley-style overhead, kaleidoscopic crane shot of the dancers surrounding Jimmy Thompson, the singer.

The final two extracts illustrate the brilliant synthesis of musical score, choreography, decor, singing, and camerawork in the "You Were Meant for Me" duet of Kelly and Reynolds and in the title song, "Singin' in the Rain." The former plays on the conventional courtship number in which Kelly's declaration of love for Reynolds is ritualized into song and dance. He develops the number by having the song and dance evolve from natural, common actions. The scene begins with their sentimental dialogue as they walk in a leisurely fashion; then Kelly states that he needs the proper setting to declare his love. So, on a spacious Hollywood set with artificial colored lights, a large fan blowing mist (to provide the right romantic atmosphere), and a musical accompaniment, Kelly sings and then both of them dance. The number is especially delightful in that it fuses the fantasy elements of the making of a film with the natural expression of love through song and dance. The lyrical rhythms of the music and the dancers, Kelly and Reynolds, are smoothly integrated with those of the camera through its tracking, dolly, and crane shots and through some invisible editing by match cutting. This tender love scene, in its stylized unreality, epitomizes the cinema's appealing world of illu-

The conventional use of musical comedy characters—Gene Kelly in eye embrace with Debbie Reynolds as buddy Donald O'Connor looks on—is found in *Singin' in the Rain.* (MGM 1952. Directed by Gene Kelly/Stanley Donen. FI)

sion, make-believe, and dream imagery appropriately set on a Hollywood back lot.

In the final extract, the title number, "Singin' in the Rain," is Kelly's visualization of spontaneous love and carefree gaiety through song and dance: it is cheerful, vigorous, energetic, and charming. He begins the scene with dialogue (as he says goodnight to Reynolds), waves the cabdriver away, walks with his umbrella, hums a few bars, sings, and then bursts into a classic, solo, spectacular dance. In contrast to Astaire who, in a dapper tuxedo, dances, usually with a partner, in a ritzy nightclub, Kelly dances alone in an ordinary suit on a city street, thus attempting to blend earthy, ordinary elements into fantasy. By taking a real-life situation and translating it into a musical fantasy, Kelly personalizes his feelings and universalizes the common man's feelings through his exuberant, unpretentiously stylized, and inventive routines. Note, for example, the manifold ways in which he incorporates the umbrella into his dance: he uses it as a cane, twirls it like a baton, dances with it as a partner, strums on it as a guitar, kicks it up into the air, flips it, sometimes uses it to ward off the rain, closes it to let the rain pour down on him, uses it to swirl with him in a huge circle around the street, and finally gives it to someone who can make more functional use of it. Again, as in the previous extract, Kelly's movements are brilliantly synchronized with the mobile camera, with film cuts of his movements, and with moments of transition in the music. The camera participates in his irrepressible joy.

The spontaneity and lyric grace of this scene are even more interesting when one learns how the scene was actually filmed. In an interview, Albert Johnson asked Kelly how the sound was achieved. Kelly replied:

> "You always do all the taps after you shoot the film because you can't hear them because of the noise on the set. You have a play-back machine: first you make a record, and you have to visualize it all in your mind and you dance back to the record. This is one of the miserable things in shooting a film; and then after you get it all shot you watch yourself on the screen and put on a pair of earphones and dub in the taps. That's the only way we've found yet to do it—it seems old-fashioned and archaic."[1]

[1] Albert Johnson, "The Tenth Muse in San Francisco," *Sight and Sound* (Summer, 1956), p. 47

This scene is masterfully conceived and executed, as is the entire film in its score, choreography, script, decor, color, acting, and comedy. Pauline Kael includes it as one of the best: "Our movies are the best proof that Americans are liveliest and freest when we don't take ourselves too seriously."[2]

Bibliography

Astaire, Fred. *Steps in Time*. New York: Heineman, 1960.

Comden, Betty, and Adolph Green. *Singin' in the Rain* (screen play). New York: Viking Press, 1972.

Croce, Arlene. *The Fred Astaire and Ginger Rogers Book*. New York: Outerbridge & Lizard, Inc., 1972.

Cutts, John. "Dancer, Actor, Director." *Films and Filming* (August/ September, 1964).

Green, Stanley. *The World of Musical Comedy*. New York: A. S. Barnes, 1973.

Green, Stanley, and Burt Goldblatt. *Starring Fred Astaire*. New York: Dodd, Mead, 1973.

Hackl, Alfred. *Fred Astaire and His Work*. Edition Austria International, 1974.

Harvey, Stanley. "Interview with Stanley Donen." *Film Comment* (July/August, 1973).

Johnson, Albert. "The Tenth Muse in San Francisco." *Sight and Sound* (Summer, 1956).

Kauffmann, Stanley, with Bruce Henstell. *American Film Criticism*. New York: Liveright, 1972.

Knox, Donald. *The Magic Factory: How MGM Made 'An American in Paris.'* New York: Praeger, 1972.

Koball, John. *Gotta Sing: Gotta Dance: A Pictorial History of the Musical*. New York: Hamlyn, 1970.

McVay, Douglas. *The Musical Film*. New York: A. S. Barnes, 1967.

Spiegel, Ellen. "Fred & Ginger Meet Van Nest Polglase." *Velvet Light Trap*, No. 10 (Fall, 1973), pp. 17–22.

Springer, John. *All Talking! All Singing! All Dancing!* Secaucus, New Jersey: Citadel Press, 1972.

Taylor, John Russell, and Arthur Jackson. *The Hollywood Musical*. New York: McGraw-Hill, 1971.

Terry, Jim, and Tony Thomas. *The Busby Berkeley Book*. Greenwich, Connecticut: New York Graphic Society, 1973.

Thomas, Lawrence B. *The Golden Age of Movie Musicals: The MGM Years*. New Rochelle, New York: Arlington House, 1973.

[2]Pauline Kael, *I Lost It at the Movies* (New York: Bantam Books, 1965), p. 72.

The Musical

Thomas, Tony. *Music for the Movies*. New York: A. S. Barnes, 1973.

Vallance, Tom. *The American Musical*. New York: A. S. Barnes, 1970.

Wigal, Don, ed. *Screen Experience, an Approach to Film*. Revised edition. Dayton: Pflaum, 1976.

Wilson, Robert, ed. *The Film Criticism of Otis Ferguson*. Philadelphia: Temple University Press, 1971.

Gene Kelly, Frank Sinatra, and Jules Munshin dance their way all over New York in one of the best of the musical genre *On the Town*. (MGM 1949. Directed by Stanley Donen/Gene Kelly. FI)

Chapter Eleven

Genre: Comedy

The two films selected for the comedy genre are *The Cameraman* (1928) by Buster Keaton and *Monkey Business* (1952) by Howard Hawks. (Several other films which were seriously considered were unavailable because permission rights for extracts could not be obtained. Among them were: *A Night at the Opera*, with the Marx Brothers; and *The Family Jewels*, with Jerry Lewis. Though we had selected and written about *The Cameraman*, permission for extracts were not secured for it. In its place we chose two extracts from Laurel and Hardy's *Hollywood Party* and *Air Raid Wardens*. See Appendix V, page 147, for details.

THE CAMERAMAN (1928) MGM

DIRECTOR: Edward Sedgwick, Jr.
PRODUCER: Buster Keaton
SCRIPT: Clyde Bruckman and Lex Lipton
CONTINUITY: Richard Schayer
PHOTOGRAPHY: E. Lessley and Reggie Lanning
EDITING: Hugh Wynn
TECHNICAL DIRECTOR: Fred Gabourie
CAST: Buster Keaton—Buster
      Marceline Day—Sally
      Harry Gribbon—Cop
      Edward Brophy—Man in bathhouse
      Harold Goodwin—Stagg
      Sidney Bracy—Editor

Cary Grant reverts to wild adolescence as he cavorts about in a sports car with Marilyn Monroe in *Monkey Business*. (Twentieth Century-Fox 1952. Directed by Howard Hawks. FI)

Plot Synopsis

Buster is a photographer who falls in love with Sally, a secretary for the Hearst newsreel company. He exchanges his tintype camera for a Pathé movie camera and vainly tries to impress her boss with his freelance work, which is a mixture of technical errors (reminiscent of the trick and fantasy shots of Georges Méliès). Nevertheless, Sally promises Buster a date for Sunday. They go to a swimming pool in Coney Island, where Buster loses his bathing suit. After they leave, Buster's rival, Stagg, drives them home—with Buster sitting alone in the rumble seat of the car. Later, Sally gives Buster a newsworthy tip: a tong war has erupted in Chinatown. Through a mixup, Buster now has an assistant, an organ grinder's monkey, to help him film the war; the assignment completed, Buster discovers that apparently he had no film in his camera.

The next day, Sally goes out with Stagg in his boat, which overturns. Buster rescues her but, when he goes for medical aid, she revives and thinks that Stagg has saved her. Meanwhile, the film of the tong war shows up at the news office, along with a film—taken by the monkey—of Buster saving Sally. Buster wins the girl and marches in a parade welcoming not him, but Lindbergh.

Extract I: 9 minutes

Sally says she will call Buster on Sunday if she is available for a date. While Buster waits, fully dressed, for her call, he tries to open his piggy bank—with destructive results. The phone rings; he races down several floors, but it is not for him. He starts back up dejectedly and ends up on the roof. The phone rings again; he races down to the cellar and then back up to the phone. While she talks, he excitedly races across New York to her boarding house and, as she hangs up, he arrives at her door. He waits for her in the waiting room with several young women and an old lady chaperone. When Sally arrives, they leave to take a double-decker bus to Coney Island. A crowd separates them, leaving Buster on the top and Sally on the bottom level. Buster climbs down and sits on the fender, only to be bumped off. He gets up, leaps onto the fender again, and rides off with his date.

Extract II: 14 minutes

This extract consists of two major scenes. In the first, Buster tries to change from his street clothes into his swimming outfit in a bathhouse cubicle already occupied by another, heavier man (Edward Brophy). In the second, Buster and Sally swim in the pool; Buster is involved in several embarrassing situations, including the loss of his bathing suit. He leaves the pool by "borrowing" the bloomers of a chubby woman. The scene ends with a man trying to pick up Sally, only to be pushed into the pool by Buster.

Discussion

The Cameraman was the first of several features that Keaton made for MGM, and possibly one of the best of all his films. Keaton never really adjusted to the MGM method of film production with its team of writers, hundreds of technicians, stars, and tight bureaucratic control which required everything to be requested in triplicate. In addition, Louis B. Mayer had no sympathy for Keaton's methods and Irving Thalberg paid little attention to his ideas about using sound. In this film for MGM, as with almost all of his previous films, Keaton worked on all phases of production: script, continuity, acting, directing, editing, and producing. And, of course, the results attest to his greatness in such films as *The Navigator* (1924), *Sherlock Junior* (1924), *The General* (1926), and *The Cameraman* (1928). Rudi Blesh, in his thorough biography of Keaton,[1] recounts the story of a friend of Keaton's who, in 1953, asked to see *The Cameraman*—only to be told that the print was worn out because MGM had used it as a model training film of comedy for its writers, actors, and directors.

This film is one of Keaton's finest because he is able to continue the development of the comic conventions that he himself helped invent: the organic story fused together by one sight gag surpassing the previous one and building to a hilarious but logical climax; Keaton's immobile, deadpan face in stark opposition to his ever moving, restless body; the vulnerable, indomitable, inventive Keaton "hero" who begins in ineptitude (in this instance, with a camera) and eventually ends in triumph; and the ambivalent use of objects, especially machines, as comic icons which first obstruct the hero and later are used by the hero to his advantage (a technique which the French critic J. P. Lebel calls "turnabout"). Keaton appeals to man's typical concern about the machine age as he confronts the machine (a motion picture camera), is overwhelmed by it at first, but eventually uses it to film a fine documentary as well as evidence of his own bravery—which results in his winning the girl. He represents the archetype of the little man who is constantly struggling to exist, and possibly triumph, in a mechanistic, senseless universe. In addition to these comic con-

[1] Rudi Blesh, *Keaton* (New York: Macmillan, 1966).

ventions, Keaton incorporates the cinema itself into his gags in this particular film. For example, he uses the two dominant fundamental approaches to film in *The Cameraman:* the Georges Méliès fantasy approach, in the first part of the film, during which Keaton makes every possible kind of photographic mistake (they are, of course, trick shots); and the Louis Lumière documentary approach of merely recording reality, during which Keaton photographs a tong war. The latter event even parodies cinéma-vérité when Keaton incites some of the action himself.

The extracts stress different elements of Keaton's comic conventions. In the first, as in most of his films, his love for a woman is his main objective and everything he does is centered on his trying to impress and win her. Keaton's body also expresses his personality. This extract, for example, stresses his restrained dynamism and concentrated energy as he sits alone, pathetically awaiting Sally's phone call. Unable to remain motionless, he tries unsuccessfully to break open his piggy bank, using both a hammer and the wall itself—which he partially destroys. In frustration and anger, he throws down the bank and, naturally, it breaks open.

When he hears the phone ring, we see him race down several flights of stairs in a marvelous parallel elevator shot. We sympathize with him when we find out the call is not for him. We laugh when, using the same structure of the stairway, he dejectedly goes up, continues onto the roof, and falls. Again, as the phone rings, he frantically bolts downstairs—only to bypass the phone and end up in a dark cellar. As Sally talks, Keaton relies on a recurrent motif in all his films: motion—especially fast, bodily motion. His race through New York traffic is a classic one: head and torso held taut and erect, eyes straight ahead, legs moving like pistons, his trajectory like a bullet: quick, concentrated, and inexorable. He arrives as Sally puts down the receiver, and apologizes, "Am I late?" His appealing shyness and reserve are revealed when he is left to wait for Sally in the waiting room at the women's boarding house.

In the bus scene, he is overwhelmed by the crowd which separates him from Sally. He then exhibits his resourcefulness by climbing down and sitting on the fender next to her. Even when he is bumped off, his tenacity, agility, and timing overcome this accident: he leaps back onto the fender again, his body nicely balanced and his face impassive, contemplative, and beautiful in repose.

In the second extract, the scene in the bathhouse is an example of how Keaton uses both space and characters inventively and

Comedy

Jerry Lewis in one of his many comic disguises clowns through *The Family Jewels*. (Jerry Lewis Productions 1965. Directed by Jerry Lewis.)

humorously. Typically, as in most of Keaton's films, he is at the mercy of the situation and, in a sense, is tyrannized by fate and a fat man as both Keaton and Edward Brophy become entangled with one another as they try to change clothes. The claustrophobic and frustrated feeling of the scene is accentuated by the static camera, which films them in a medium shot, surrounded by the three walls of the restricted cubicle.

The swimming pool scene plays again on Keaton's style. His awkward reserve with women develops into confusion and embarrassment as Sally is surrounded by other men: he falls into deep water; he never catches the ball when she throws it to him; in trying to impress her, he dives into the water and loses his bathing suit; then, naked, he is surrounded by playful girls; and then Sally wants to leave the pool for the beach. But, as usual, he is ever resourceful—he ducks underwater, strips off a fat lady's bloomers, and escapes. The extract ends on a triumphant note. When Keaton returns, a he-man is trying to pick up Sally. Keaton tricks him by dropping a handkerchief; as the man gallantly bends over to pick it up, Keaton's fragile self-confidence becomes more assertive and he kicks the man into the pool. Keaton, throughout the film, not only uses a variety of sight gags, but is able to transcend them through his disciplined and expressive humanity.

MONKEY BUSINESS (1952) 20th Century-Fox

DIRECTOR: Howard Hawks
PRODUCER: Sol C. Siegel
SCRIPT: Ben Hecht, Charles Lederer, and I.A.L. Diamond; based on a story by Harry Segall
PHOTOGRAPHY: Milton Krasner
MUSIC: Leigh Harline
EDITOR: William B. Murphy
ART DIRECTOR: Lyle Wheeler and George Patrick
CAST: Cary Grant—Barnaby Fulton
    Ginger Rogers—Edwina Fulton
    Charles Coburn—Mr. Oliver Oxley
    Marilyn Monroe—Lois Laurel
    Hugh Marlowe—Harvey Entwhistle
    Robert Cornthwaite—Dr. Zolbeck
    Joseph Mell—Barber
    George Eldredge—Auto salesman

Plot Synopsis

An absent-minded research chemist, with a seemingly happy marriage, is preoccupied with discovering a drug to restore youthful vigor. Although he is unable to combine the correct ingredients, a laboratory chimpanzee does so—then pours the formula into the laboratory water cooler. The main body of the film then deals with the funny but disastrous results of Professor Fulton and his wife Edwina's knowingly drinking the formula. The first time they take it, they revert to the teenagers they would have liked to have been; the second time, they unknowingly take an overdose and revert to savage children. By the end of the film, even the minor characters have taken the drug, which releases all their suppressed impulses; finally, however, order is restored.

Extract: 14 minutes

Professor Barnaby Fulton continues to work on his formula to restore youth. When he leaves the laboratory for a few moments, a chimpanzee escapes from its cage, accidentally mixes the correct formula, then pours it into the water cooler. Fulton returns, devises his own formula, acts as his own guinea pig by drinking it, then washes it down with the "real" formula from the water cooler. As a scientist, he notes his reactions: a sense of extreme well-being, no need for glasses, and no bursitis.

He then goes on a wild youth binge: he gets a youthful haircut; buys a dapper suit and argyle socks; purchases a racy convertible sportscar, and, of course, meets a sexy young woman, Lois Laurel (Marilyn Monroe). With her in the car, he speeds around—getting into two accidents—with interludes at a skating rink and a swimming pool before the formula wears off.

Discussion

This film is a revival of one of the major American forms of comedy—the "screwball" comedy, stressing the male vs. female relationship so popular in the 1930s. "Screwball" comedy developed with the introduction of sound into the movies, and is characterized by an emphasis on fast-paced dialogue; cynical, wisecracking humor; social satire; the absurdity of life in a madcap world; a frantic but tightly structured plot; and a lack of respect for the Establishment. Visually, the genre features mostly medium shots; straight, simple cuts; and no dissolves or flashbacks. Some of the better examples are such films as Lewis Milestone's *The Front Page* (1931); Frank Capra's *It Happened One Night* (1934) and *You Can't Take It With You* (1938); Gregory La Cava's *My*

Man Godfrey (1936); W. S. Van Dyke's *The Thin Man* (1934); and Preston Sturges' *The Palm Beach Story* (1942). Probably the best examples, however, are Hawks' comedies: *Twentieth Century* (1934); *Bringing Up Baby* (1938); *His Girl Friday* (1940)—a remake of *The Front Page* with Hildy Parks, now transformed into Hildy Johnson, played brilliantly by Rosalind Russell; *Ball of Fire* (1941); and *I Was a Male War Bride* (1949).

Monkey Business (1952) employs the consistent motifs that run through several of Hawks' comedies while simultaneously remaining staples of American comedy: the painful and humorous appeals of the "id" unleashed in marriage; the confusions and splits within individuals' identities; and the "Fountain of Youth" myth of a magic elixir capable of rejuvenating man—all of which are expressed in a frenetic, slapstick style. Drinking the formula "B-4" is the catalyst for all Hawks' characters in this film to rip down the façade of their adult personae and let loose their suppressed desires, especially those which were sexually inhibited during the character's adolescence and adulthood. Once Hawks establishes the credibility of that premise, he relentlessly pushes it to its logical but brutal conclusion: men and women reverting to atavism and barbarism.

He achieves this result in such a way, however, that it arouses ambivalent responses in his audience. One is simultaneously attracted to and repulsed by witnessing the foolish degradation of another human being (a theme most recently touched upon in the popular *Planet of the Apes*). The contradictions center on the character reversal/regressions of Professor Barnaby Fulton and his wife Edwina, which merge grotesqueness with humor, primitivism with civilization, instinct with reason, infantilism with maturity, shame with laughter, and embarrassment with insight. Hawks explodes the romantic illusion of William Wordsworth that man, by returning to the state of childhood and infancy, is at his best and that, as he grows older, he loses that pristine purity of birth. Instead, Hawks shows man abandoning himself to violent and ugly forces.

Still, these savage forces have a fundamental allure to man, as can be seen in Robert Louis Stevenson's *Dr. Jekyll and Mr. Hyde.* In both Mamoulian's version of the Jekyll-Hyde story and Hawks' *Monkey Business*, man proudly presumes to alter his very nature, with tragedy the result for Jekyll and comedy for Barnaby Fulton. One can find elements of this obsession with man's conflict between primitivism and civilization in many of Hawks' films encompassing a variety of genres: the gangster film, in *Scarface;* the

Western, in *Red River;* the comedy, in *Bringing Up Baby;* the war film, in *Sergeant York;* the detective film, in *The Big Sleep;* and the science fiction film, in *The Thing.*

In the extract itself, the contradictions between control and abandonment are much in evidence. The intelligent and dedicated professor is seen working calmly on a formula for man's betterment. Ironically, it is a non-intelligent monkey which parodies Barnaby by accidentally concocting the correct mixture. The mixture, of course, shows Barnaby not so much as he really was in his adolescence, but rather unleashes exactly those actions which he was too inhibited to perform then. Barnaby undergoes a complete reversal of his normal behavior patterns. From a sexual point of view, this reversal is explicitly shown when he immediately recognizes Lois Laurel (Marilyn Monroe) just by seeing her legs beneath a sign. In a previous scene, as the staid professor, he closely examines her nylons (which he invented) but does not notice her obvious beauty. And again, in the extract's driving scene, when she asks him if his motor is running, he replies : "Is yours?"

Hawks displays not man's primeval innocence, but his rampant regression to a baser order, by carefully cataloging Barnaby's humiliating screwball antics: he belly flops into a pool after stupidly asking, "Is everybody watching?" (Who in their right mind would watch him with Marilyn Monroe in a swimsuit nearby?) He careens wildly in a skating rink and drives dangerously in a fast sportscar, only to climax the scene by crashing the car for the second time.

Yet Hawks attempts to balance these actions with an emphasis on the sheer exuberant joy and humor the characters experience after sampling the youth-restoring drug. Barnaby enjoys the temporary feeling of freedom the formula gives him from the restricting roles he plays as professor, intellectual, and husband: he no longer feels suppressed or enclosed by his job, society, and marriage. Hawks himself has said, in an interview about the film: "The laughs are born out of inhibitions that restrict each of us and are here removed by rejuvenation." Possibly the laughter borders on tragedy, because of the resulting painful recognition as we see ourselves in Barnaby.

The extract is a good example of Hawks' comic style: the camera is unobtrusive; the editing is smooth, with an orderly building up of shots based on variations of the theme of Barnaby's silly actions; the pace and dialogue are hectic and rapid; and the two sexually attractive stars, Grant and Monroe as they cavort in slapstick roles, are delightfully presented.

Bibliography

Agee, James. *Agee on Film*. New York: Beacon Press, 1966.

Barnes, Peter. "Cuckoo" *Films & Filming*, August, 1960. (on Laurel and Hardy)

Barr, Charles. *Laurel and Hardy*. Berkeley: Univ. of California Press, 1968.

Baxter, John. *Hollywood in the Thirties*. New York: A. S. Barnes, 1968.

Bishop, Christopher. "The Great Stone Face" and "An Interview with Buster Keaton." *Film Quarterly*, XII (Fall, 1958), pp. 10–15 and 15–22.

Blesh, Rudi. *Keaton*. New York: Macmillan, 1966.

Bogdanovich, Peter. *Cinema of Howard Hawks*. New York: Museum of Modern Art, 1962.

Brackett, Leigh. "A Comment on the Hawksian Woman." *Take One*, Vol. 3, No. 6 (July/August, 1971), pp. 19–20.

Brownlow, Kevin. *The Parade's Gone By*. New York: Ballantine Books, 1969.

Casty, Alan. *Development of the Film*. New York: Harcourt, Brace, 1973.

Durgnat, Raymond. *The Crazy Mirror*. New York: Delta, 1969.

Everson, Wm. K. *The Films of Hal Roach*. New York: Museum of Modern Art, 1971.

_____. *The Films of Laurel and Hardy*. New Jersey: The Citadel Press, 1967.

Farber, Manny. *Negative Space*. New York: Praeger, 1971.

Gilliat, Penelope. "Buster Keaton." *Film 70/71*. Ed. D. Denby. New York: Simon and Schuster, 1971.

Grierson, John. "The Logic of Comedy" in *Grierson on Documentary*. New York: Harcourt, Brace and Company, 1947.

Haskell, Molly. "Howard Hawks: Masculine, Feminine." *Film Comment*, Vol. 10, No. 2 (March-April, 1974), pp. 34–39.

Hawks, Howard. "Interview." *Take One*, Vol. 3, No. 8 (November/December, 1971).

Kaminsky, Stuart M. *American Film Genres*. Dayton: Pflaum, 1974.

Keaton, Buster, and Charles Samuels. *My Wonderful World of Slapstick*. Garden City, New York: Doubleday, 1960.

Kuhns, William. *Movies in America*. Dayton: Pflaum, 1972.

LaHue, Kalton C. *The World of Laughter*. Norman, Oklahoma: Univ. of Oklahoma Press, 1966.

Lebel, J. P. *Buster Keaton*. New York: A. S. Barnes, 1967.

Buster Keaton is again at the mercy of a mechanical object in his best film, *The General.* (Buster Keaton Productions-United Artists 1927. Written and directed by Buster Keaton. A-B)

Maltin, Leonard. *Movie Comedy Teams*. New York: New American Library, 1970.

Maltin, Leonard, editor. *The Laurel and Hardy Book*. New York: Curtis, 1973.

Mast, Gerald. *The Comic Mind: Comedy and the Movies*. New York: Bobbs-Merrill, 1973.

McBride, Jim. *Focus on Howard Hawks*. Englewood Cliffs, New Jersey: Prentice-Hall, 1972.

McCabe, John. *Mr. Laurel and Mr. Hardy*. New York: Doubleday, 1961.

McCaffrey, Donald W. *The Golden Age of Sound Comedy*. New York: A. S. Barnes, 1973

McCaffrey, P. W. *Four Great Comedians*. New York: A. S. Barnes, 1968.

McCreadie, Marsha, ed. *The American Movie Goddess* (on Marilyn Monroe). New York: John Wiley and Sons, 1973.

Mellen, Joan. *Marilyn Monroe*. New York: Pyramid, 1973.

Montgomery, John. *Comedy Films*. London: Geo. Allen and Unwin, 1954.

Parish, James Robert. *The Fox Girls* (M. Monroe) New Rochelle, New York: Arlington House, 1971.

Perkins, V. F. "Hawks' Comedies." *Movie Reader*. Ed. Ian Cameron. New York: Praeger, 1972.

Phillips, Gene. *The Movie Makers: Artists in an Industry*. Chicago: Nelson Hall, 1973.

Robinson, David. *Buster Keaton*. Bloomington: Indiana University Press, 1969.

_____. *The Great Funnies*. New York: Dutton, 1969.

Rubenstein, E. *Filmguide to the General*. Bloomington: Indiana University Press, 1973.

Sadoul, Georges. *Dictionary of Filmmakers*. Berkeley: University of California Press, 1972.

Sarris, Andrew. *The American Cinema: Directors and Directions 1929–1968*. New York: Dutton, 1968.

_____. *Interviews with Directors*. New York: Bobbs-Merrill, 1967.

Shipman, David. *The Great Movie Stars*. New York: Bonanza Books, 1970.

Sypher, Wylie, Henri Bergson, and George Meredith. *Comedy*. Garden City, New York: Doubleday, 1956.

Vermilye, Jerry. *Cary Grant*. New York: Pyramid, 1973.

Wead, George. "Keaton: The Carpenter as Artist." Chicago *Sun Times. Midwest Magazine* (March 11, 1973), pp. 35–40.

Comedy is fused into the detective genre with William Powell, Myrna Loy and, of course, Asta in *The Thin Man* series. (MGM 1934. Directed by W. S. Van Dyke. Screenplay by Albert Hackett and Frances Goodrich from the Dashiell Hammett novel.)

Wise, Naomi. "The Hawksian Woman." *Take One*. Vol. 3, No. 3 (January/February, 1971), pp. 17–19.

Wollen, Peter. *Signs and Meaning in the Cinema*. Bloomington: Indiana University Press, 1969.

Wood, Robin. *Howard Hawks*. Garden City, New York: Doubleday, 1968.

Appendix I

The Use of Extracts in Film Teaching

by Daniel Millar, of the Department of
Film and Television, Bede College, Durham, England[1]

The increasing interest in film teaching in schools and in further education has led to a greater availability of materials, including extracts from feature films, usually selected by, and rentable from, the British Film Institute (81 Dean St., W.1). Most of these are 10–20 minutes in length, and a substantial minority are beginnings or endings of film, or else sequences, like the Odessa Steps extract from *The Battleship Potemkin*, which have a unity in themselves. Even so, it is desirable that the teacher using an extract should have seen the whole film, though occasionally he may decide to put himself on a level with his students and work "blind" on an extract from a film he does not know. Even when he knows the film well, he should confine most of his discussion to the extract itself, if only to avoid the just irritation of the students. But anyone who has used practical criticism methods in teaching literature will be familiar with the problems and will have evolved his own ways of meeting them.

Extracts have been used in many different approaches to film teaching, so a broad distinction should here be made between the contextual method and film teaching in the stricter sense. The first uses film, among other illustrative materials, to teach a broader

[1] Daniel Millar, "The Use of Extracts in Film Teaching," *English in Education* (British), Vol. 2, No. 1 (Spring, 1968), pp. 17–23.

subject such as social studies or English or general studies; and it has become associated, by oversimplification, with Kingsway Day College, where much of the pioneering work was done, not only with this approach, but also in film teaching proper. The second type treats film as a subject in itself or in association with other media, such as television or perhaps drama. And it is in this area that the extract, as a teaching tool, seems to be on the decline in popularity and prestige just when considerable efforts in negotiation with film distributors have at last made a wide and varied range [of extracts] available. So the main purpose of this article is to suggest that the extract, despite real limitations, still has considerable value in film teaching, and should not fall into disuse.

Use of Extracts as a Teaching Tool Declines

First, why the decline? One cause may be the increasing emphasis on the work and personality of the individual director, deriving from the *politique des auteurs* of *Cahiers du Cinéma*, the originality of which consisted mainly in treating certain American directors at least as seriously as European *auteurs*. Another may be the greater interest in genres which has accompanied this rediscovery of American cinema. For both these approaches, the whole film, as exemplar of style or type, is clearly preferable to the extract. At the same time, other approaches, for which the extract was more obviously useful, have declined from their formerly central positions. These are the "grammar of film" method, which analyses technical elements separately to build up a fuller "appreciation" (itself a dated word) of the sum effect; and the historical, which shows the development of the medium from Lumière to Godard. Both [of] these can, perhaps must, use extracts to make specific points or just to cover the ground.

The new orientations away from grammar and history to *auteur* and genre seem to me improvements both critically and pedagogically, and roughly parallel well-established developments in teaching literature—in fact Dr. Leavis might be surprised to find that his is the most commonly quoted name in current theoretical discussion, though not much of this has so far filtered into print. Extracts still can have a use in *auteur* and genre teaching, as well as in other ways, and the rest of this article will outline, with examples, what these are.

Auteur Criticism Defined.

First, the *auteur* approach. This assumes that one man, the director, is responsible for the total effect of a film, *e.g.*, that the merits and defects of *Torn Curtain* are attributable to Hitchcock rather than to Brian Moore, the sole credited scriptwriter (or Paul Newman and Julie Andrews either). Examples are legion, especially in French, and almost any issue of *Sight and Sound* will yield one discussion of a director. The method may be described as "admiring explication": a good full-length instance is Robin Wood's *Hitchcock's Films* (Zwemmer, 1965); and my own essay "Godard's World" (*Screen Education*, No. 38, March/April, 1967) indicates its orientation even in the title. Teachers of literature will find this mode of criticism almost dangerously congenial and easy to handle, but provided they are aware of, yet not overawed by, the complexities of the filmmaking process, no harm will result. In fact, young people who accept that *somebody* wrote a poem or story are remarkably unwilling to believe in any controlling hand behind a piece of film or television, no matter how extended the credits. So even over-emphasis has its initial virtues.

Three obvious uses of the extract in *auteur* teaching are:

1. To introduce or revise a full showing of a film. Since discussion will spread out from the extract or focus more sharply into it, both the film itself and the chosen part should be rich in significance, and a middle section is better than a beginning or ending. The best examples I have used are Buñuel's *Los Olvidados*, Lang's *The Big Heat* and Wajda's *A Generation*. Within English cinema, Schlesinger's *A Kind of Loving*, Clayton's *The Pumpkin Eater* and Anderson's *This Sporting Life* also are viable, and, on a different tack, can be used in conjunction with extracts from the original novels.

2. To show the variety or development in one director's work. Here again the extract is supplementary to the showing of a whole film. Convenient pairs might be Wajda's *A Generation* and *Ashes and Diamonds* or Antonioni's *L'Avventura* and *L'Eclisse*. These are oddly parallel examples in that each can be worked both ways (in fact, there are two extracts from *L'Eclisse*, the beginning and the end), each starts and finishes a trilogy, and each instances a development from realism to baroque which is arguably growth or decay (or, to be boringly uncontroversial, simply change). In working out such not-so-easy problems in the classroom, a teacher may learn much about his students' tastes and temperaments and something about his own.

3. To quote in single lectures or short courses where the director's work is already well-known. This is more appropriate to adult or extramural teaching, where the group is self-selective, than in schools or further education. It might be made to work for

a few directors, such as Hitchcock and Ford,[2] who recur on television as well as in the local cinemas; but it is best to sound out the ground first, and anyway this is not a game for beginners.

These three ways with *auteur* criticism are not exhaustive, since they exclude comparison, one of the most fruitful extensions of the directorial approach, as I hope to show later. Once again, any literature teacher who uses both set books and comparative practical criticism will find the analogy obvious enough, especially if he has started off by clipping out excerpts from the prescribed texts for preliminary practical criticism exercises.

Genre Films: the Western

Next, genre cinema, a topic too large and controversial, as well as fascinating, to deal with properly here. Genre is traditionally associated with American cinema, particularly the Western, the gangster, the musical and possibly the war film. The distinguishing feature of a genre is that it operates within a set of conventions, evolving yet recognisable, which create audience expectations within, or sometimes against, which the film works. Each genre has a virtually distinct history, and the flexible interplay between the formal requirements of a genre and the personal vision of an individual director offers very rewarding study. While this is best done with whole films where possible, extracts can help to summarize the history of a genre and to make individual points effectively.

Take, for instance, the sharp contrast in the use of violence between Ford's *Stagecoach* and Anthony Mann's *The Man from Laramie*, impersonal in Ford, almost sado-masochistic in Mann. The characters in *Stagecoach* are readily recognisable classic types, even within the extract (the chase of the stagecoach across a salt plain by the Indians); and when Donald Meek gets an arrow through him, this seems as much a part of the ritual as redskins tumbling from the saddle or the rescuing cavalry charge. But when James Stewart is deliberately and vengefully shot through the gun hand, we feel the pain and see the blood (like most modern Westerns, *The Man from Laramie* is in colour, so blood is bright red rather than dark grey). There is also some psychological analysis of the bad guy, the spoilt and petulant son of a domineering father, before the extract ends with his being shot by a

---

[2] Seven Ford extracts are available (including two from *She Wore a Yellow Ribbon*) and they run from *The Informer* (1935) to *Two Rode Together* (1961), a fair span. Of the four Hitchcock extracts, only one *(Foreign Correspondent)* is familiar, so their usefulness is limited.
   (Additional note, 1973: Further extracts have been made from Hitchcock's films, including *Mr. and Mrs. Smith, Shadow of a Doubt, Under Capricorn, Psycho, The Birds.)*

fellow gun-runner. More interestingly, Mann's fascination with the rocky landscape of the West emerges in the opening gunfight, which is comparable with the final gun-battle in *Winchester 73;* but Mann's tendency to the baroque and grotesque is more marked in *Man of the West,* with its peculiar divisions of loyalties, ghost town shoot-up, and bizarre rape of Julie London by Lee J. Cobb.

This baroque development in the Western, which appears also in Arthur Penn's *The Left Handed Gun,* reached an early high point in Nicholas Ray's *Johnny Guitar* with its sado-lesbian overtones and strange use of colour (for instance, red is dominant in the extract, compared with [the] usual greens and browns of the West). Some French critics admire it, and the Godard's Pierrot le Fou sent his house-maid to see it because it was "good for her education." Certainly it exemplifies a Western so personal and even eccentric that it ceases to be more than nominally a genre film (just as the same director's *Party Girl* can hardly be helpfully described as a gangster film).

At the other end of the scale, even the extract from Delmer Daves' near-documental *Cowboy,* which is concerned with painstaking evocation of a setting and a style of life, has its bizarre touch in the unexpected death by snakebite resulting from a practical joke. But at least Daves is consistent in that [the] tragedy arises naturally out of the desert fauna, whereas the monsters of Ray and, to a smaller extent, of Mann are within the mind. It may be useful to discuss with students whether the so-called "Psychological Western" is a necessary and inevitable development (if only because of TV Westerns) or a distortion of classic form.

The Gangster Film

The Western is immediately recognised by any age of student, whereas the gangster film is a hazier genre, shading off into other films of crime like murder mysteries and even the spy film. Nowadays young people may be more familiar with the half-hearted reconstructions of *The Untouchables* than with the occasional Cagney or Bogart movie that crops up on TV. Perhaps the issue is further complicated in that the hero-figure may be a gangster or reformed criminal or alternatively an investigator, such as a policeman or a private eye. In fact, this almost exactly parallels the Western; but it creates a greater problem, because the setting in place and time is more flexible in the gangster genre. So it is helpful to start with three extracts which suggest the ethos, style and a little of the history of the type, namely *Little Caesar, The Maltese*

Falcon and *The Harder They Fall*. The first shows the odd mixture of theatricality and abrupt violence of the films made when prohibition and the big gangsters it produced were still contemporary. The second, more sophisticated in style and dialogue, belongs to the private eye period of seedy offices and ironic wit; it features a comic and occasionally violent exchange between Humphrey Bogart and Peter Lorre. The third, *The Harder They Fall*, really belongs to a fringe sub-genre, the boxing film, which the director, Mark Robson, had previously helped to create with *Champion*. But the opening sequence, shot on location in New York and easily the best part of the film (before Budd Schulberg's earnest script takes over), evokes beautifully the grimy grandeur of the big city, the tense excitement of fast cars, the sense of danger as tough-looking types converge at a dreary rendezvous, the training-gym, looking forward to easy and illegal money. The extract ends with the battered face of Bogart, an archetypal figure in his last film, lighting his cigarette with a characteristic tough-guy gesture.

These extracts are best followed by a full-length masterpiece of the genre such as Lang's *The Big Heat* (or possibly Huston's *The Asphalt Jungle*, if it is available). To this I would add Kubrick's *The Killing*, a taut and originally constructed *hommage* (especially in its use of actors) to the genre; and also a more personal and unconventional *hommage*, Godard's *À Bout de Souffle*. The extracts from *The Big Heat* and *À Bout de Souffle* can be used as introductions or, better, recapitulations. If they have to be shown on their own, some additional explanation may be necessary. For instance, the *Big Heat* extract shows Bannion (Glenn Ford) investigating at a wrecked car lot which, though evocative in itself, takes on added force when we know that he is looking for the men who planted a bomb in his car, killing his wife. Similarly, when Vince (Lee Marvin) burns a bargirl (Carolyn Jones) with his cigar, this not only echoes the sadistic murder of Lucy Chapman earlier in the film, but also foreshadows the scalding of Debbie (Gloria Grahame) with a pot of boiling coffee. Yet the tensions and subtleties of attitude among the gangsters, and in the exchanges of Bannion with the lot owner and then with Vince, are interesting enough to be worth analysing even out of context, and give some hint how Lang can infuse so much moral and human feeling into a relatively conventional though well-articulated plot. The extract from *À Bout de Souffle* is the opening of the film and shows Michel (Jean-Paul Belmondo) ditching a girl-friend in Marseilles, stealing a car, shooting a policeman on the way, stealing

128   Appendix I: Film Teaching

from another girl-friend in Paris, and finally reencountering a third girl, the American Patricia (Jean Seberg), to whom he gives a smooth line of patter about the good life they could have in Italy. While this demonstrates Michel's cynical, anarchic side (as well as Godard's free-wheeling way of adapting the gangster tradition) it only touches on the romanticism of his essentially hopeless love for Patricia and of his equally hopeless imitation of the Bogarthian tough-guy image in a hard, real (and French) world.

Other Genres and Themes

There is no space here to touch on other genres, such as the musical, or to say much about the thematic approach, into which it can shade, as in the war film—where one can even identify other national genres besides the American, such as British, Polish, Russian and perhaps Italian. Anyway the B.F.I. Education Department (81 Dean St., W.1) issues a useful pamphlet called "Some Suggested Themes and Materials" which groups extracts, shorts and features under a dozen headings. Another pamphlet, "Film Teaching Material," lists not only extracts but also six Study Units, organised round such themes as War, Young People, and Imprisonment, and usually consisting of a feature and several extracts. These can be rented for a month or six weeks at a time, which allow detailed study. But they are often heavily booked, up to a year ahead, and it may be more practical to organise one's own study unit on similar lines, even if this means hiring the feature on two occasions several weeks apart.

Extracts Used for Analysis and Comparison

Besides the *auteur*, genre, and theme approaches, there is a fourth way in which my colleagues and I have found extracts useful—as an introduction to a fairly protracted block of film study, which covered documentary and other types of film as well as features. It seemed necessary to have an introductory session on the "Language of Film," the way film works, while yet avoiding too grammatical a method and concentrating on directorial control. A recent list was:

> *The Battleship Potemkin*
> (Eisenstein)
> *A Man Escaped*
> (Bresson)
> *Ashes and Diamonds*
> (Wajda)

Appendix I: Film Teaching   129

The Maltese Falcon
(Huston)
The Eclipse (Extract A)
(Antonioni)
The Pumpkin Eater
(Clayton)

This gave us three [films] loosely connected with war, one genre film, and two on personal relationships. These could be worked in several ways, but I shall conclude with only one example, comparing *A Man Escaped* (1956) with *The Eclipse* (1962), both extracts being the beginnings of the films.

A Man Escaped

The Bresson extract shows Fontaine (Françoise Leterrier) being taken to Gestapo H.Q. in Lyon by car, unsuccessfully attempting escape on the way, and being beaten up. Locked in a cell, he signals to the man in the next cell by tapping on the wall and talks to Terry (Roger Tréherne), one of three prisoners allowed the comparative freedom of exercise in the courtyard and having outside contacts. [This freedom] enables [Terry] to get pencil and paper, pass on letters to Fontaine's family and Resistance group, and send up a safety pin with which Fontaine can undo his handcuffs, following instructions from his unseen neighbour.

Apart from a few sparingly used long shots to clarify the geography (or geometry) of events, this extract, like most of the film, is built on a series of faces, hands and objects, such as the gear lever which will signal the moment for attempted escape, the gun butt and clubs which punish failure (the actual gun shots seem almost irrelevantly casual, since we know from the title that Fontaine *will* live to escape, and from common sense that he can't escape *yet*), the handkerchief which mops up blood, the other handkerchief which serves as a basket slung from the cell window, the handcuffs which confine and yet tap messages through the wall, the pencil and paper which communicate with the outside world (inevitably reminiscent of *Diary of a Country Priest* visually, though the function is different), the pin which creates the first move towards freedom.

This intense and equal concentration on faces, hands and objects increases the sense of place and of confinement within closed spaces—the car, the interrogation room, the cell—without resorting to the almost heavy-handed (by Bresson's standards)

Appendix I: Film Teaching

emphasis on opening and closing doors in *The Trial of Joan of Arc*. A particularly clear instance is the first escape attempt, where the camera remains within the car, focussed unremittingly on the immobile yet completely expressive face of the other prisoner, while the external action is off in a corner of the frame, half-seen through the window. If this seems at first an almost self-consciously classical treatment of violence, it is immediately counteracted when, still in the same shot, Fontaine is shoved back into the car and efficiently clubbed unconscious with a gun butt. He bows his head in a gesture both self-protective and accepting, a slight movement which suffices to tell us that his next attempt will not be quick and impulsive, but careful, long-mediated and, after this harsh lesson, successful. (This one shot also demonstrates very concisely how much the early Godard owed to Bresson, most obviously in *Le Petit Soldat*.)

The grey, documentary photography of the opening sequence sets a tone for the whole film, which we only gradually come to recognise as an effect of austere and functional beauty. Perhaps this needs to be said explicitly, since it may not be obvious from the extract alone. The beauty of the film is not *only* spiritual or in what it "says" about the human soul; it is actually present on the screen and in the sound track. But it is inextricable from meaning and expressiveness; no one is likely to say, "It was a lousy movie, but the photography was good" (a form of reaction which unfortunately becomes increasingly meaningful as each year goes by).

The sound track is as restrained as the visuals; opportunities for conversation are occasional and brief. As the pictures are mainly faces, hands and objects, the sounds are mainly commentary (by Fontaine), sound effects and silence. Later on there will be rather more conversations, though not many, and even some music (a Mozart Mass), but not much.

Yet, in a sense, the construction of the film itself is as much musical as narrative. It works by repetition, variation, enlargement. The theme of isolation and self-sufficiency is beginning to be played against that of trust in others and help from them—apparently contradictory, yet both necessary. This quasi-dramatic theme is echoed in the very texture of the film by the contrast between Fontaine's still face and his unflaggingly determined eyes (in an interview with Godard in *Cahiers du Cinéma* Bresson not surprisingly expressed his admiration for the art of Buster Keaton), or again between the face that gives nothing away to his captors and the hands which busily yet unhurriedly work away at the goal of freedom. Bresson picked up the latter visual theme in his next film, *Pickpocket,* giving it there a much more ironical but also obscure treatment, whereas *A Man Escaped* has a transparent clarity which makes it more successful as art and, incidentally, much more suitable for teaching.

The Eclipse

Antonioni's *The Eclipse* begins with an almost self-contained episode, the end of a love affair between Vittoria (Monica Vitti) and Riccardo (Francisco Rabal), and it is this sequence, preceded by the main titles, which forms Extract A (Extract B is the famous "documentary" final sequence, which I shan't discuss here). It makes its effect in two different ways: first, it is meant to have behind it the weight of the analysis of feelings in *L'Avventura* and *La Notte,* the two previous films in the trilogy; secondly, it creates dramatically the state of emotional and spiritual impasse from which Vittoria spends the rest of this film trying to escape, temporarily or unsuccessfully.

Perhaps it is this double pressure on a brief episode that brings it close to the self-parody which some critics have found in it. Certainly it lacks the full creative freedom of some later episodes in the film (Vittoria's happier moments) or the experimentation of the final sequence; but its peculiarly weighted, almost ponderous concentration imposes its own emotional discipline on the viewer, so that what on first screening seems boringly inactive becomes, the second time, almost too full of visual clues. These take two forms, what is seen and how it is seen—which at once differentiates this extract from the Bresson, where such a distinction does not consciously arise, even in the escape attempt shot just quoted. To put it another way, an art director would be very busy working for Antonioni and almost unemployed with Bresson. (This, of course, is only a way of expressing critical points for students, not at all a reference to the history of individual films, which would be far too technical, probably unavailable and ultimately irrelevant.)

Comparison of the Films

Whereas Bresson showed an action, Antonioni is creating a situation, so that lack of progression is part of the *donnée.* Not that the scene lacks movement in any sense; Vittoria's nervously languid walking about the room is more than matched by the camera's fluid searching for fuller information and varied compositional relationships—the dolly shot is as essential to Antonioni's style as it is startling in Bresson's (*e.g.,* Joan's walk to the stake in

The Trial of Joan of Arc, brilliantly re-echoed by Marie's night walk in *Au Hazard Balthazar*).

This is one reason why, though much of the meaning is carried in both extracts by objects, faces and stillness, Antonioni's is quite different in effect from Bresson's. There are others. First, Giovanni Fusco's sombre, powerful music over the credit titles (themselves plain white on black, yet elegantly modern) sets a mood even before the opening shots give it a specific reference. Secondly, objects are not isolated but cluttered in the spacious (though, in an emotional sense, also cell-like) room, which gives an impression of expensive luxury. Riccardo is a left-wing intellectual, perhaps an editor or publisher (maybe even a writer, like Giovanni in *La Notte*), but he lives in a richly modish style. Thirdly, Vittoria herself is, in the opening sequence, a beautiful and expensively dressed decoration. Like the other objects, she has a degree of independence and self-sufficiency; she is capable of motion within a tethered range, but so is the whirring fan that precedes her restless pacing.

Whereas Bresson uses *things* to express human purpose, need or frustration, so that they take on spiritual significance through function, Antonioni shows things as apart, indifferent or only expressive of mood (*e.g.*, the overflowing ashtray). Indeed, people sometimes seem at the mercy of things, like the mushroom tower which appears when the curtains are drawn back—students quickly spot the phallic overtones, but it is also threatening in its dominance and in its echo of the mushroom cloud which overhangs modern life. Similarly, the cluttered books and *objets d'art*, though individually expressive, are cumulatively encroaching and chaotic, as if Riccardo is overwhelmed not so much by possessions as by his education, by ideas and abstractions, so that he falls back on cliché in matters of feeling—he is virtually saying, "If our love has died, let's get married!" (The analysis of sentiment here, while thoroughly Italian, has almost a Lawrentian ring, though the negative side of Lawrence.)

Another point of apparent similarity and actual divergence between Bresson and Antonioni is their fondness for setting a human figure against a bare wall. Why are the results so different that they hardly even seem comparable? Again, it is partly the difference between "action" and "situation." Whereas Bresson's figures are actively expressing a state of soul in very specific terms through interior monologue, Antonioni's are either silent or vaguely attempting to communicate some general comment on a state of mind. The difference is also partly in lighting and subjects. Bresson's walls are grey and drab, Antonioni's are dazzling white (or, in later films, a striking pastel colour). Clothes look second-hand in Bresson, highly fashionable in Antonioni. Bresson's people are interesting-looking, while Antonioni's are good-looking. Feelings harden in Bresson, but deliquesce in Antonioni.

Perhaps one can hint, even on the basis of these two extracts, why Bresson is ultimately a greater and more cinematic director than Antonioni—certainly a more classical director, whereas Antonioni's apparent intellectual toughness in the analysis of emotions comes closer to sentimentality and fashionable cynicism.

No one could be less world-weary than Fontaine, who is highly aware of and responsive to human contacts, ties and responsibilities. He is essentially an agent, whereas Vittoria and Riccardo, as translator and editor (or whatever), are at one remove from first-hand experience. Compare Riccardo and Fontaine as each slumps wearily in a scruffy shirt. Clearly Riccardo is the more pitiable, yet it is Fontaine who has blood on his face, handcuffs on his wrists. . . .

All this, of course, makes Antonioni a more *modern* director, and not only because he is portraying the present and Bresson, the past. Bresson is no less interested in spiritual states, but ties these closely with a *plot*, a straight line of action off which the reflections develop—a plot perhaps more Aristotelian than Hollywoodian, but nonetheless perceptible. With Antonioni the plot is minimal and mood becomes paramount—even more obviously in his next film, *The Red Desert* (though in *Blow-Up* he returned to plot and strict form, so that it might be argued this is *structurally* a more classical film than its four predecessors). Rather than follow through this slightly specious point, I would rather conclude by suggesting that Bresson's most recently shown film, *Au Hazard Balthazar*, makes a far more profound and shocking comment on modern life than anything Antonioni can find in "swinging" London.

I have deliberately taken these speculations well beyond the limit of what one normally can attempt in the classroom. In doing so, I hope to have suggested that the extracts can provide a springboard as well as a locus for analytic comparison. At the more mundane level where we usually work, while awaiting the days of the Film Tripos and the Honours School in Cinema, perhaps the modest claim that relatively unsophisticated students will find a short extract easier to assimilate than a whole Bresson or Antonioni film may seem more realistic. If so, this only emphasises the wide range of possibilities for the use of extracts.

Appendix II

Specific Techniques Used in Film Study Course
(sample films are listed in parentheses)

1. View film; "image-skim," *i.e.*, ask for specific images that seem to stand out, for one reason or another, to the student; no "wrong" answers build up the student's confidence in seeing film and his willingness to articulate. (*The Searching Eye*)

2. View film; discussion; view entire film again; discussion of whole film (*Citizen Kane*) or selected scenes (*King Kong*) (any other feature)

3. View film; no discussion; written responses in the form of brief phrases (what's your emotional reaction?) or formal essays (a five paragraph critical-evaluative essay). (*Phoebe*)

4. View film; no discussion; thinking and pondering. (*Summer We Moved to Elm Street*) (*Good Night, Socrates*)

5. View film; form panels of 10, with chairman and secretary, but without teacher; chairman and secretary report the consensus of group's discussion to entire class. (*Phoebe*)

6. View film; select one scene from film and discuss in depth. (*On the Waterfront*) (*Citizen Kane*) (*No Reason to Stay*)

7. View film; role-playing of characters in film. (*High Noon*) (*Silent Snow, Secret Snow*)

8. View a number of films; no discussion of any until all have been shown; evaluate how each develops an idea through visualization. (any documentary)

9. View a number of films; students keep a journal of their responses to films.

10. View film with sound turned off to stress visuals and suggest sound track. (*Fiddle-De-Dee*) (*A Time Out of War*) (*The Critic*)

11. Record sound track and listen to it before viewing film; see if class can create content which is suggested by music; view film. (*Dream of the Wild Horses*)

12. View film in parts; stop film after major scenes or sequences; discuss foreshadowing, style, microcosm of whole film. (*Citizen Kane*) (*Last Laugh*)

13. Considering just one film, collect on paper selected comments from various critics which are at odds or extremes with each other. First, have the students give their own critical response to the film; compare these with the critics' notes. Discuss differences with supporting evidence from the film. (*Taking Off*) (*On the Waterfront*) (*Bonnie and Clyde*) (*The Graduate*)

14. Lectures: on styles, movements, directors, writers, genres, or actors. (John Huston, Akira Kurosawa, the New Wave, Neo-Realism, Russian film industry, McLuhanism, the Western, Marlon Brando)

15. Discussion-lecture by film critics; students prepare questions.

16. Filmmakers discuss their films. (Invite upper class or former student filmmakers)

17. Panel of students acting as film critics to discuss one specific film, series, or outside film.

18. Panel of students and teachers to discuss one film. (*High School*) (*No Reason to Stay*)

19. Read story or script first; discuss; view film; compare-contrast forms. (*Silent Snow, Secret Snow*) (*Night and Fog*)

20. View film; discuss; read story and script; discuss. (*The Informer*) (*Of Mice and Men*) (*The Grapes of Wrath*) (*Woman of the Dunes*)

21. View film; distribute evaluation sheet on one film, the entire unit, and the teaching method.

22. View film; write visualization of ideas or words in similar style, technique, or form as a treatment. (*Enter Hamlet*) (*Oh, Dem Watermelons*)

23. Cut up a comic book story, frame by frame; arrange the individual frames on a larger piece of paper; and describe the distance from which each frame is viewed (long shot, close-up); angle from which it is seen (above, below); why it is larger, smaller or a different shape than other frames; what it tells about the story; how it connects with the frame before, and moves the reader to the next frame, etc.

24. With an abstract idea in mind, *e.g.*, violence, collect 10 individual photographs from newspapers and magazines; try to arrange them in a *meaningful* sequence, Scotch-taping them across the backs and pulling them across an overhead projector. Explain the reasons for your arrangement.*

25. Take the same or another abstract idea; make a script—a series of notes on subject, sequence and treatment—for another 10-image form. This time, take your own photographs with a camera so that you have control over lighting, distance, focus angle, composition, etc. While assignments 23 and 24 are concerned with forming (or editing) given material, as in the cutting room, this assignment indicates that editing or montage (from the French word for "arrange") begins with the concept and permeates to every part of the creative or formative process.*

26. Carefully record the sequence of images, subject by subject, of the short film *Dream of the Wild Horses;* then try to create a parallel form, in prose or poetry or a combination of the two.

27. From a series of pages in a magazine, photographs of a series of billboards, Burma-Shave placards, etc., illustrate an advertisement which is a sequence of signs; explain its motivational structure.*

28. Submit a proposal for teaching four or more children something about how series of images work, something about how to see, or how to explore the visual environment.*

29. Write a visual script for a one-minute advertisement for something; produce it on videotape, using props, live actors, painted posters, and other kinds of materials.*

30. Write a script for a five-minute slide-tape show. In addition to other elements, you now will have control of color, which can be used significantly or symbolically, and of time and rhythm, as well as of the matching of sound to image.*

31. Filmstrips and/or slides of specific shots from films (*e.g.*, *Citizen Kane* or *The 400 Blows*, available from "Understanding the Art of Film," Educational Dimensions Corporation, P.O. Box 126, Stamford, Connecticut 06904) can be used for close analysis of *mise en scene* elements (lighting, composition, etc.)

32. Use stills or slides from a film (film catalogs often have photos) so that the class can set the scene by recalling situations, character motivation, tone, mood, dialogue, music.

33. Use stills or slides from a film to study the use of icons in a particular genre. (guns and cars in gangster films like *Public Enemy* and *Little Caesar*)

*This suggestion comes from Professor Gerald O'Grady, Department of English, State University of New York, Buffalo, New York 14214.

34. Compare/contrast two films on differing sets of values. (*Sean*) (*What If the Dream Comes True?*) (*Sixteen in Webster Groves*) (*Taking Off*) (*The 400 Blows*)

35. Record narrative elements of a film's sound track, replay it, and discuss how it might be visualized. Then look and listen to the sound track with visuals to see how literary elements are adapted to film. (Orson Welles reading the first few paragraphs in *The Magnificent Ambersons* or the narrative in *Silent Snow, Secret Snow*)

36. Record two to four minutes of music from the sound tracks of five to ten films over a unit or semester. At the end of the unit, replay the tracks and have the class jot down: 1. what visuals from the film they recall; and/or 2. what images or feelings the sound tracks elicit.

37. Use "image-skim" technique to have entire class recall significant or most impressive images. As these are listed on the board, the students are "replaying" the film. When a number of images have been listed, discuss such elements as structure, organization, style and rhetoric of the entire film; changes and development in character, theme, camera movement, lighting, transitional techniques, and point of view. (*War Game*)

38. Choose one scene from a film; draw a storyboard of significant shots, with stick figures, for close analysis of composition and movement.

39. View a short film for close analysis; retell the film by listing each scene and/or shot in the order in which it is shown. (*One Week* by Keaton)

40. Compare/contrast two films on the use of propaganda techniques. (*Triumph of the Will*) (TV commercials, which often are available free from the advertisers)

41. Videotape the proceedings of one class; use it as one example in a discussion of *cinéma vérité* techniques and the characteristics of a documentary. (objectivity, point of view, hand-held camera, recording/shaping of reality, personal/social significance)

Most of the above techniques are discussed in detail in *Film in the Classroom*, by Ralph J. Amelio (Pflaum/Standard, 2285 Arbor Blvd., Dayton, Ohio 45439, $4.75).

Appendix III

A List of Film Distributors

A-B   Macmillan Audio Brandon
         8400 Brookfield Avenue
         Brookfield, Illinois 60513
         (312) 485-3925

BFI   British Film Institute
         Education Department
         8 Dean Street
         London, England WIV 6AA
         (extracts not available in
         U.S.A., but catalogs are)

C   Contemporary Films/McGraw-Hill
         1221 Avenue of the Americas
         New York, New York 10020

CFS   Creative Film Society
         7237 Canby Avenue
         Reseda, California 91335

EG   Em Gee Film Library
         4931 Gloria Avenue
         Encino, California 91316

FI   Films Incorporated
1144 Wilmette Ave.,
Wilmette, Ill. 60091
(312) 256-4730

IFB   International Film Bureau, Incorporated
332 South Michigan Avenue
Chicago, Illinois 60604
(312) 427-4545

LCA   Learning Corporation of America
711 Fifth Avenue
New York, New York 10022

MPC   Metromedia Producers Corporation
8544 Sunset Boulevard
Hollywood, California 90065

MMA   Museum of Modern Art Film Library
11 West 53rd Street
New York, New York 10019
(212) 245-8900

PYR   Pyramid Films
P.O. Box 1048
Santa Monica, California 90406

ST   Sterling
241 East 34th Street
New York, New York 10016
(212) 683-6300

TFC   Teaching Film Custodians, Incorporated
25 West 43rd Street
New York, New York 10036
(212) 695-1640

TEX   Texture Films
1600 Broadway
New York, New York 10019

T-L   Time-Life Films
43 West 16th Street

New York, New York 10011
(212) 691-2930

TWY   Twyman Films
329 Salem Avenue
Dayton, Ohio 45406
(513) 222-4014

UCE   University of California Extension Media Center
University of California
Berkeley, California 94720

WB   Warner Brothers/7 Arts
4000 Warner Boulevard
Burbank, California 91503
(213) 843-6000

W-P   Willoughby-Peerless
115 West 31st Street
New York, New York 10001

Appendix IV

Recommended Periodicals for Film Study Course

American Cinematographer
ASC Agency, Inc.
1782 North Orange Drive
Hollywood, California 90028
Monthly—$6.00/year

Catholic Film Newsletter
Suite 4200
405 Lexington Avenue
New York, New York 10017
Twice-monthly—$8.00/year

Cinefantastique
Box 270
Oak Park, Ill. 60303
Quarterly—$8.00/year

Cinema
9667 Wilshire Boulevard
Beverly Hills, California 90212
Tri-yearly—$5.00/year

The Critic
American Federation of

142

Film Societies
333 Avenue of the Americas
New York, New York 10014
Nine issues—$5.00

Film Comment
1865 Broadway
New York, N.Y. 10023
Six issues—$9.00

Film Heritage
Wright State University
Dayton, Ohio 45431
Quarterly—$2.00/year

The Film Journal
Box 9602
Hollins College
Roanoke, Virginia 24020
Quarterly—$5.00/year

Film Library Quarterly
Film Library Information
Council
Box 348
Radio City Station
New York, New York 10019
$8.00/yearly

Film News
Film News Company
250 West 57th Street
New York, New York 10019
Six issues—$6.00

Film Quarterly
University of California Press
Berkeley, California 94720
$5.00/year

Filmfacts
P.O. Box 213
Village Station

New York, New York 10014
Semi-monthly—$35.00/year

Filmmakers Newsletter
P.O. Box 46
New York, New York 10012
Monthly—10 issues/$5.00

Films and Filming
Hansom Books
Artillery Mansions
75 Victoria Street
London, England SWIH OH2
Twelve issues—$14.00

Films in Review
National Board of Review of
Motion Pictures, Inc.
210 East 68th Street
New York, New York 10021
Ten issues—$8.50

Journal of Aesthetic Education
1002 West Green Street
Urbana, Illinois 61801
(Two special film issues:
July, 1969, and April, 1971—
$2.50)

Journal of Popular Film
University Hall 101
Bowling Green State University
Bowling Green, Ohio 43403
Quarterly—$4.00/year

Literature/Film Quarterly
Salisbury State College
Salisbury, Maryland 21801
$6.00/year

Media and Methods
134 North 13th Street
Philadelphia, Pennsylvania

19107
Nine issues—$5.00

Monthly Film Bulletin
British Film Institute
81 Dean Street
London, England WIV 6AA
$6.80/2 years

Screen
Society for Education in Film
and Television
63 Old Compton Street
London, England WIV 5PN
$7.00/year

Sight and Sound
Eastern News Distributors, Inc.
155 West 15th Street
New York, New York 10011
$6.00/year

Sneak Preview
National Educational Film
Center
Route 2
Finksburg, Maryland 21048
Eight issues—$7.00

Take One
Unicorn Publishing Company
P.O. Box 1778, Station B
Montreal, Canada H3B 3L3
Bi-monthly—$4.50/12 issues

Variety
154 West 46th Street
New York, New York 10036
Fifty-two issues—$20.00

Velvet Light Trap
The Arizona Jim Co-op

Old Hope Schoolhouse
Cottage Grove, Wisconsin
53527
Quarterly—$3.00/year

An excellent resource book which concisely describes the types of articles the above periodicals contain is *Magazines for Libraries*, by Bill Katz and Barry Gargal (New York: R. R. Bowker and Co., 1972). See also *Current Film Periodicals in English*, compiled by Adam Reilly, Educational Film Library Association, 17 West 60th Street, New York, New York 10023. (Revised edition, January, 1972)

Appendix V

Changes in the Extract Program

Because of unavoidable complications, Films, Inc., was unable to secure final permission on two of the extracts: *The Cameraman* from the Comedy Unit and *Singin' in the Rain* from the Musical Unit after these had been selected, cut, and described both on cassette tapes and in this book. In fact we were not allowed to extract any other MGM musical in place of *Singin' in the Rain*, presumably because of the success of *That's Entertainment* in June, 1974, a fine documentary on the many MGM musicals. Thus we were unable to use as substitutes *On the Town, An American in Paris, Meet Me in St. Louis, Anchors Aweigh, Brigadoon*, or other fine MGM musicals.

Therefore, we turned to the 20th Century-Fox and Paramount musicals and chose first *Call Me Madam*, but finally settled on *Funny Face* from Paramount for the final musical selection. For the comedy unit we chose extracts from two Laurel and Hardy films: *Air Raid Wardens* and *The Hollywood Party*.

FUNNY FACE (1956) Paramount

DIRECTOR: Stanley Donen
PRODUCER: Roger Edens
SCRIPT: Leonard Gershe based on the Gershwin Broadway show
PHOTOGRAPHY: Ray June, John P. Fulton

COLOR PHOTOGRAPHY SUPERVISOR: Richard Avedon
CHOREOGRAPHY: Fred Astaire, Eugene Loring
ART DIRECTION: Hal Pereira, George W. Davis
COSTUMES: Edith Head
EDITOR: Frank Bracht
MUSIC: Arranged by Adolphe Deutsch from George and Ira Gershwin, Roger Edens, and Leonard Gershe
CAST: Dick Avery—Fred Astaire
    Jo Stockton—Audrey Hepburn
    Maggie Prescott—Kay Thompson

Plot Synopsis

High fashion magazine publisher Maggie Prescott (Kay Thompson) desires a new face to model for a Paris designed collection of clothes in her next issue. Her top photographer, Dick Avery (Fred Astaire), discovers hidden possibilities in a shy, intellectual, Greenwich Village book clerk Jo Stockton (Audrey Hepburn). He sees in her face "character, spirit, and intelligence." She agrees to model for "The Quality Woman" collection for the magazine only because it means a trip to Paris where she hopes to talk with her idol, Professor Flostre, who specializes in "empathicalism." While in Paris, she enjoys both the city and her modeling job but even more her photographer. When Dick Avery warns her of the Professor's non-philosophic and amorous intentions toward her, she becomes angry with Avery only to have him proved correct. Both Hepburn and Astaire then dance happily together as the film ends.

Extract I: (5 minutes)

As Jo is trying to escape from the magazine staff who want to revamp her as the model "Quality Woman," she hides in the dark room where Dick Avery is developing photographs of her face. When she learns that he recommended her, she puts down her funny face, which leads to Avery's song and dance "Funny Face." The scene ends with a close-up of Jo's beautiful face.

Extract II: (8 minutes)

After a whirlwind week of Avery shooting Jo all over Paris—museums, fountains, streets—they arrive in a churchyard garden to photograph the final dress of the collection, a lovely wedding dress. Jo doesn't want the week to end; she says she loves Paris, the clothes, the garden, and Avery. Avery is happily stunned by her confession and he responds with both song and dance, "He Loves, She Loves."

Discussion

Funny Face is a good example of the tradition of the musical based on the Broadway stage success, which peaked in the fifties and sixties. Musicals derived from Broadway included *Oklahoma, Carousel, The King and I, South Pacific, Bye Bye Birdie, Gypsy, My Fair Lady, The Sound of Music, Camelot, Oliver, Sweet Charity* and *Hello Dolly.*

Fred Astaire stands out as the best example of one who has merged his creative talents with the musical genre as it had developed from the escapist depression thirties, through the war-torn forties, to the placid fifties and the chaotic sixties. Both extracts from *Funny Face* (1956) provide a number of significant examples indicating the major changes between the musical genre of the thirties and the fifties. Most obvious, of course, is the use of color. In the "Funny Face" title number, red integrates the musical number into the logical setting. This color dominates the scene as it provides both the correct setting for Dick Avery as a photographer developing her pictures and an appropriate atmosphere for the "developing" romantic relationship between Dick Avery and Jo Stockton. Red is used throughout the entire scene, but the final shot is an impressive, contrasting close-up of Audrey Hepburn's face in sharp black, white, and flesh tones. In the "He Loves, She Loves" number, the blues and greens, softened by gauze over the lens, transform the scene from the reality of a simple churchyard into the fantasyland of a handsome prince and his princess.

The character that Fred Astaire plays is quite different from the debonair, tuxedoed, man-about-town in *Gay Divorcee* and other thirties' musicals. Here he is a photographer dressed in casual clothes, a light blue sweater and grey slacks in one number, a raincoat with umbrella in another. The emphasis here is on the ordinary, average guy. No longer is he a dancer by profession, using nightclubs, dance halls, and Broadway stages as his settings. Instead we see him in a confining darkroom in one scene and an expansive churchyard in another. In both cases the natural settings are logical and functional to the development of the plot.

As in most Astaire musicals the motivation for the numbers arises out of a romantic situation. While Jo Stockton belittles her funny face, Astaire gradually and lyrically convinces her of her beauty: as he develops her photographs into larger and larger close-ups, he begins to sing a solo, music then comes in, he dances first alone and then briefly with her, and finally ends the number singing alone. Whereas in the musicals of the thirties, where Astaire developed the love motif in virtually every dance number with his partner Ginger Rogers, this film reflects more stress on Astaire's individual contributions as a dancer, teaming with Hepburn only in portions of two numbers.

The "He Loves, She Loves" number—a typical courting routine—reflects the combined talents of the entire musical team, actors, director (Stanley Donen), cinematographer (Ray June), costumes (Edith Head), editor (Frank Bracht), and orchestra. The scene is richly romantic. The newly discovered love of Avery for Jo dressed in a white bridal gown is sensitively ritualized into song and dance, almost totally a duet. The dance is brilliantly accomplished through the graceful movements of Astaire and Hepburn, the integrated participation of the camera through smooth tracking shots, dollying in and out, and the final slow boom shot as the lovers also move away from the camera, and the fluid cutting of the shots to the music. The natural, spacious, and verdant surroundings of trees, lakes, flowers, grass, swans and birds set the stage for the ritual love ceremony as Astaire and Hepburn spontaneously reflect their happiness through dance. (This same setting is used to end the film when Astaire and Hepburn sing a duet to "S'Wonderful.")

THE HOLLYWOOD PARTY (1934) MGM

DIRECTORS: Richard Boleslavsky, Allan Dwan, Roy Rowland
PRODUCERS: Harry Rapf and Howard Dietz
SCREENPLAY: Howard Dietz and Arthur Kober
MUSIC AND LYRICS: Rodgers and Hart, Arthur Freed, Gus Kahn
PHOTOGRAPHY: James Wong Howe
CAST: Stan Laurel—Himself
     Oliver Hardy—Himself
     Jimmy Durante—Schnarzan
     Lupe Velez—Herself
     Charles Butterworth—Harvey Clemp
     Polly Moran—Henrietta Clemp
     and many others

Plot Synopsis

Hollywood movie hero Schnarzan gives a huge party to try to secure the sale of ferocious lions for his next big picture. Laurel and Hardy crash the party. Of course, the party ends in chaos as the lions break loose.

Extract: (4 minutes)

Definitely the best part of an uneven all-star musical revue, the egg-breaking scene is one of the classic routines created by Laurel and Hardy over a long and successful history of funny situations. Their antagonist is the fiery Latin Lupe Velez, who stands off Laurel and Hardy only to be finally humiliated when she sits down on an egg that Stan Laurel has placed on her chair. (Part of this situation was reworked into *The Bullfighters* in 1944 with Margo Woode in the Lupe Velez role.)

AIR RAID WARDENS (1943) MGM

DIRECTOR: Edward Sedgwick
PRODUCER: B. F. Zeidman
SCENARIO: Martin Rackin, Jack Jeune, Charles Rogers, Harry Crane
PHOTOGRAPHY: Walter Lundin
CHARACTERS: Stan Laurel—Himself
Oliver Hardy—Himself
Edgar Kennedy—Joe Bledsoe, citizen and moving man
Horace/Stephen McNally—newspaper editor Eustace Middling
Donald Meek—Nazi spy
Jacqueline White—Peggy Parker, reporter

Plot synopsis

After Laurel and Hardy are rejected by the local World War II draft board and are out of work, they become air raid wardens at home. They bumble their way through most of the film only to foil a plot by enemy spies to sabotage a magnesium plant.

Extract: (6 minutes)

Laurel and Hardy as air raid wardens dutifully trudge off to make certain that no houselights are visible during the night. They meet one homeowner, Edgar Kennedy, who is unaware of the warning and unwilling to adhere to their demands. The scene ends with Laurel and Hardy wrecking his entire house.

Discussion of Both Extracts

The extracts are from among the few Laurel and Hardy sound features available from Films, Inc. Yet, they are representative of several of the characteristics of the comic style of Laurel and Hardy over their illustrious career from 1917 to 1951 with over a hundred films (short and feature).

Basically both extracts take a conventional situation with a dispute or confrontation and then stylize it by escalating the conflict into chaos and destruction, or what John McCabe, in his biographical study of the team, calls "reciprocal destruction." In the scene from *The Hollywood Party* Lupe Velez bops Ollie with her shoe and then calmly drops a raw egg on Stan's shoe. They, of course, follow in their tradition by retaliating instantly. Stan begins by breaking an egg in her shoe. Using a minimum of props, they develop this theme with variations on eggs as weapons. However, these weapons fulfill an essential function of Laurel and Hardy's comedy—as each side increases its inventive use (misuse) of the eggs, so also is there a decline in the dignity of the characters, especially the antagonist of Laurel and Hardy. As slapstick comedians they exhibit their mastery of the art of puncturing the dignity of a character and a situation. Here, of course, the beautiful Lupe Velez' pride is deflated when, ultimately, she sits on the egg in a duel of oneup (or down) manship.

The *Air Raid Wardens* extract is similar in its use of mutual destruction except here there is much more physical movement from room to room and more use of props. In this scene, Laurel and Hardy are effectively reunited with a member of the old Hal Roach stock company, Edgar Kennedy, the master of the exasperated slow burn. He is allowed ample opportunity to use his stock-in-trade as he vainly attempts to prevent the inevitable demolishing of his house. In these two extracts, Laurel and Hardy continued their tradition made famous in such earlier scenes as the melee of pie throwing in *The Battle of the Century* (1927), the destruction of the automobiles in *Two Tars* (1929), and the ruination of James Finlayson's house in *Big Business* (1929).

In both extracts, the careful attention to small details, the simplicity of the situation, snowballing pace, the comic timing are other obvious characteristics of their style. Typical of most of their features, the scenes have little relationship with the rest of the plot. Probably the most crucial elements of their comic spirit, however, are the characters themselves, not only the physical contrasts of the fat Ollie and thin Stan or their marvelous, funny faces which have an appealing visual quality, but more their endearing warmth, childlike innocence, and engaging naiveté. They maintain their popularity because as a team they portray an elemental and universal humanity in confronting the world on their own terms and surviving its absurdities.

Appendix VI

Extracts Available

The following extracts, under the series title *American Film Genre*, are available from Films Inc. (see Appendix III, Distributors). Each extract unit is accompanied by a cassette tape lecture by Stuart M. Kaminsky and a film genre study guide.

The Horror film
Dr. Jekyll and Mr. Hyde (1952) (15 min. b/w extract)
King Kong (18 min. b/w extract)
Lease $337.50   Rental $40

The Science-Fiction film
The Day the Earth Stood Still (12 min. b/w extract)
The War of the Worlds (20 min. color extract)
Lease $447.50   Rental $40

The Gangster film
Murder, My Sweet (12 min. b/w extract)
St. Valentine's Day Massacre (12 min. color extract)
Lease $319.50   Rental $40

The Western film
My Darling Clementine (14 min. b/w extract)
The Gunfighter (15 min. b/w extract)
Lease $297.50   Rental $40

The Musical film

Funny Face (12 min. color extract)
The Gay Divorcee (18 min. b/w extract)
Lease $379.50   Rental $40

The Comedy film

The Laurel and Hardy Compendium
  Air Raid Wardens (12 min. b/w extract
  Hollywood Party (4 min. b/w extract)
Monkey Business (14 min. b/w extract)
Lease $307.50   Rental $40

Index